AF228087

God's Ultimate Plan

Uncovering the truth of Jesus and his mission

God's Ultimate Plan

Uncovering the truth of Jesus and his mission

JOHN R. CLARKE

Copyright © 2023 by John R. Clarke

All rights reserved. No part of this book may be reproduced or used in any manner without written permission of the copyright owner except for the use of quotations in a book review.

For more information, contact: memoir433@gmail.com

978-1-80541-151-2 (paperback)
978-1-80541-152-9 (ebook)

This book is dedicated to our Heavenly Father, the Almighty and everlasting God, to our Lord and Saviour Jesus Christ, and to the blessed anointing of the Holy Spirit, who is our comforter and teacher. May you, the reader, receive grace and peace and find many blessings among the pages of this book. I also dedicate this book to my wonderful wife, Kalpna, and our son, Sam. Both are great gifts and a blessing from God. This book is also dedicated to every believer in Jesus Christ our Lord, and with the wish that God will bring you great blessings through the reading of this book.

Contents

Preface

There has been much talk and discussion as we approach the end of this age about what all religions have in common and whether this common ground be exploited to make a single religion. Indeed, there have been conferences to discuss how this can be achieved to bring Christianity under a single umbrella. However, in order to do this, everything must be removed from Christianity that is offensive to other religions. Therefore, it is more important than ever to reiterate what is unique to our Christian beliefs and, above all else, that Jesus Christ is our Lord and Saviour. There is no other name in heaven by which we may be saved from the coming anger of God. We have received the Spirit of God so that we may know what God has freely given to us. Christ crucified is a stumbling block to the Jews and foolishness to all those who have not entered the Kingdom of God. In this book, I have outlined and discussed the uniqueness of Christ and expounded on God's purposes for His Kingdom on the earth in the last days of this age and on His Kingdom in the world to come. I have also shown who we are in Christ and have reminded us that we are God's treasured possession and all that means. We are all on a journey with God, and I trust that this book will aid you in finding your place on that journey. I hope this book will be a great blessing to all who read it.

John R. Clarke

God is light; there is no darkness in him

In the beginning, when God created the heavens and the earth, the earth was void of anything, dead and empty full of darkness (see Genesis 1:1). Then, through the power of His Holy Spirit and as He spoke the word, God separated the light from darkness (see Genesis 1:3-4). Having separated the light from the darkness we see that God is light, there is no darkness within him at all (1 John 1:5). If God is light, and we as believers in Jesus as the Lord and Messiah are called to be holy as God is holy, then we should reject the darkness and walk in the light. Indeed, if we continue to walk in the darkness, then we deceive ourselves, and God's truth is not within us (1 John 1:6). So, we need to decide if we are going to walk in the light or if we are prepared to stay in the darkness.

Jesus is the light of the world

Jesus is the light of the world, and whoever follows Jesus will be delivered from walking in the darkness and will forever be part of the light that leads to eternal life (John 8:12). Jesus has overcome the darkness, which is the world dominated by Satan (John 1:5). As long as Jesus is in the world there was light, and yet there is a time coming when darkness will overtake the world (John 9:4-5). We, as

Christians, are called to walk in the light and on the road that Christ set up for us, and to become children of the light (John 12:35-36).

Those who are evil prefer the darkness because it can hide their evil deeds for a time (John 3:19-20). There is much talk between Christian scholars pertaining to comparative religion and looking at what we have in common with other religions, particularly the monotheistic religions of Judaism, Islam and Christianity. However, we should be looking, in these dark days, not at similarities between the religions but at what makes Christianity unique. What do we have that no other religion has, for that is the basis of our faith?

Only through Jesus do we have a life that is illuminated (John 12:46) and has a purpose and meaning. This is the claim of Christianity that sets it apart from all other religions and cults. There is no other name under heaven through whom a person can be saved from the coming wrath of God (Acts 4:12). No other religion is able to show the way to eternal life apart from the Gospel message. What must we do to have eternal life? Jesus is the way to God. He provides the truth that is needed to grasp and understand our purpose for being in the world. Jesus also provides the hope and the future that is eternal life beyond the grave (John 14:6-7). The good news of the gospel is that everyone who calls on the name of the Lord Jesus shall be saved from the coming wrath of the just and perfect Almighty God and shall have eternal life (Romans 10:13). Have you accepted Jesus into your heart and your life? As the darkness of the world grows and moves toward the end of this age, now is the time to open our eyes and be assured of our faith.

Seek, and you will find

Isaiah calls upon us to seek the Lord while he may be found and to call for his help while he is still nearby (Isaiah 55:6). There will be a time when the Lord will withdraw and can no longer be found by men and women. It is vitally important that we seek the Lord while he is here to be found. All those who do not know the Lord their God and Jesus as their Lord and Saviour are doomed to eternal damnation and to remain in darkness for eternity (Luke 13:27-28).

The most important question in life is, *"Where will you spend eternity?"* There is no other question that comes close to this question. Many Biblical scholars today do not believe in heaven and hell. The argument, in part, is how can a loving God possibly send anyone to a godless eternity where there will be much suffering, weeping and gnashing of teeth? However, the gospel message is that Almighty God is a God that cannot tolerate sin or evil. Therefore, those who remain in the darkness, that is, everyone who has rejected Jesus Christ as their Lord and Saviour, will have no grounds of appeal or any grounds to be saved. God demands atonement for our sins, and He has provided a sacrificial lamb in the person of Jesus Christ to take the place of our sins. Jesus is the lamb of God who takes away the sins of the world (John 1:29). The wages or payment for our sins is death and an eternity in the darkness where there is no hope of salvation (Romans 6:23).

The Bible tells us that many are called to be in the Kingdom of God, but few are chosen because mankind has mainly rejected the salvation that God has freely offered through His Son Jesus Christ (Matthew 22:11-14). If people refuse to repent and believe in

Jesus Christ as their Lord and Saviour, then they will perish in God's eternal fire of hell.[1]

The righteous who have Jesus as their Lord and Saviour are called to seek the Kingdom of God and God's righteousness, and God promises to add everything to our experience and our needs (Matthew 6:33).

How should we respond?

For those whose hearts and minds are set on Jesus, the author and perfector of our faith, or if you prefer, the source or foundation of our faith (Hebrews 12:2), then Jesus tells us to be wise and build the house of our life on the rock of his word. However, not only build on the word but put into the practice the word of God (Matthew 7:24-27).

The good news is that in a world of ever-increasing darkness, we have a great light to show us the way through the darkness (Isaiah 9:2). Jesus is our wonderful counsellor, our mighty God, our prince of peace (Isaiah 9:5). The day is fast coming when Jesus will return to establish and implement justice, and there will be everlasting peace (Isaiah 9:6). We need to open our eyes and see what the signs and times are showing us. It is time to arise and shine, for our light is here, and the glory of the Lord is rising upon His people (Isaiah 60:1). However dark the world is, the Lord, through the Holy Spirit, has arisen on each one of us who believe and trust in Him (Isaiah 60:2). We are promised that nations will be drawn to the light of Jesus as it is exhibited through His faithful people (Isaiah 60:3).

---

1   A. W. Tozer. Born After Midnight. Chapter 3. Faith is a journey, not a destination, page 18. Christian Publications, Inc. Pennsylvania, USA. 1959.

Never in the history of mankind do the nations need to see the light coming into our generation, which is the glory of God coming down from on high. In the United Kingdom, there are high fuel prices, and people are despairing about how they are going to keep their families warm this winter. The high fuel prices are parallel to increasing food prices, and many families will have to juggle staying warm with feeding themselves. On top of this, there is an additional strain of high inflation and increasing mortgage costs, with many people struggling to keep a roof over their heads. Also, many people struggle to pay heir rent as landlords put up prices to cover their costs. The Bank of England is raising interest rates to try and bring down inflation which is at a 50-year high of over 10%. In addition to this, there are an ever-increasing number of people coming to our shores, seeking asylum from tyranny in their own countries. One estimate has been that over 28,000 people arrived in the UK in the first few months of 2022, and they keep coming looking for a better life. Politicians are being criticised for stating that we are being invaded and that the asylum system is broken. It is easy to see that the Government has no answers to the rising challenges that are occurring on a daily basis in our country.

The only solution to our problems and difficulties is Jesus. There is an urgent need in our country for an outpouring of the Holy Spirit - a need for people to turn back to God. There is a critical need for people to come to repentance and leave their evil ways. They need to return to the Lord so that He can have mercy upon them and bring a profuse, generous and bountiful pardon (Isaiah 55:7-8). There is a serious and grave need to proclaim the word of the Lord to the free nations while there is time because the clock is ticking, and the day of the Lord is rapidly coming before us. God promises that His word shall not return to Him empty-handed but will accomplish everything He intended it to achieve (Isaiah 55:11).

God calls us to buy bread and milk without money or cost to us, and if we listen to God, we will delight in rich food and be able to eat what is good (Isaiah 55:1-3). This is undoubtedly a message for our times; it is a message that the people of the Western free world desperately need to hear now. The good news is that if we repent and return wholeheartedly to God, then God promises that we will go out with joy and return to a peaceful life, and we shall go forth with songs of joy (Isaiah 55:12). Furthermore, instead of struggling with rising prices and thornbushes of inflation, high fuel, and increasing food costs, we will find affordable costs of living (Isaiah 55:13). We can be assured that God will be a light to our feet so that our darkness is lit up (Psalm 119:105; Psalm 18:28). This provides us with confidence that we are walking in the ways of the Lord because there is a constant voice behind us saying, *"This is the way of the Lord, walk in it."* (Isaiah 30:21)

Responsibilities of believers

We are the light of the world, and as such, we need to be beacons that light the way for those who are stumbling in the darkness (Matthew 5:14-16). We are called to declare the mighty acts of God to those who are living in darkness (1 Peter 2:9). The church today has lost this vision of proclaiming the gospel to the world. We are too scared to cross the line and be the light that we are called to be. We are too wrapped up with our mission statements and church policies to see that world is in darkness and the people in darkness are heading for the precipice of eternal judgement and damnation. Our nation is sleepwalking into catastrophe after catastrophe as the people of God stay silent. We are called to give light to those who are dwelling in darkness and in the shadow of God's judgement (Luke 1:79).

As children of the light, we are called to stay awake and watch what is happening in the world (1 Thessalonians 5:5). We need to be surveillant and watchful; be alert and not taken by surprise at the events that the people of our country are facing (Luke 21: 34-36). It is dangerous to be unaware of what is happening in the world around us because we could be caught in the trap that the Lord of darkness is preparing for all mankind. We can become complacent about what is happening and fail to heed the many warnings that God is providing for us. Paul warned us 2000 years ago that the night is far gone and the day of the Lord's return is nearer now than it was on the day when we first believed in Jesus as our Lord and Saviour (Romans 13:11-13). It is noteworthy that both Luke and Paul warn believers against getting drunk. We are also warned not to be drawn into depravity and vice, promiscuity and arguing with each other.

People falling out with each other within churches is among the saddest failures of the Christian witness. It is divisive and reduces the effectiveness of the Christian witness within the local or national region. A.W. Tozer points to the tragedy of wasted religious activity, where people simply waste an hour in church or in a prayer meeting, where churches pray the same prayer every week without any expectation of the prayers being answered.[2] Tozer alludes to the fact that there are people who have been Christians for decades but have failed to grow in the faith and remain as children of God rather than adults in the faith.[3] People pray to the Holy Spirit to change them and help them to grow without ever having the belief that anything will happen.[4] We may not be able to control our circumstances, but we can command our response to our circumstances, and this is where the battle can be won in our daily living.[5]

Our struggle is against the powers of darkness

We are in a battle with the forces of darkness for the souls of our friends, family, colleagues, those who live in our neighbourhood, and for the centre of our countries (Ephesians 6:12). Satan has organised his army of followers into the spiritual forces of evil, and he has his rulers over countries, regions and evil spiritual forces in the heavenlies. We know that these spiritual forces can oppose the will of God, and it is up to us believers to take command and overcome the plans of the evil one (Daniel 10:13-15).

We should be aware that those who are in darkness have had their eyes and minds blinded to the truth of the gospel of the glory of God (2 Corinthians 4:4). We should be careful who we link up with in our daily lives. While we are called to be witnesses of Christ and

2   A. W. Tozer. Born After Midnight. Chapter 24. The tragedy of wasted religious activity, pages 100-101. Christian Publications, Inc. Pennsylvania, USA. 1959.

3   IBID, pages 100-101.

4   IBID, pages 102-103.

5   A. W. Tozer. Born After Midnight. Chapter 15. Accepting the universe, page 65. Christian Publications, Inc. Pennsylvania, USA. 1959.

shine our light into the darkness, we must be aware that there cannot be fellowship between those who are in the light and those who are in the darkness (2 Corinthians 6:14). Be careful what we watch or see because our eyes can easily be deceived and corrupted. If our eyes are healthy, then our whole body will be full of light (Matthew 6:22-23). We should be careful not to be deceived by empty promises or words as we must live as the children of the light (Ephesians 5:6-8). It is important to note that some people are so full of evil that they are beyond redemption (Jude 1:13). Let us not partake in the fruitless works of darkness but focus on what is pleasing to the Lord and Saviour whom we serve as children of the light (Ephesians 5:8-15). We should be wise in how we live, and this part of the Christian life is missing in many Christians in the so-called free society of the Western world today. If we are to get closer to God and to stand in His holy place, then we must have clean hands and a pure heart to seek the face of our God (Psalm 24:2-6). Let the King of Glory enter our hearts and fill our minds with His purpose for our life; then, we can walk in victory (Psalms 24:7-10).

Prayer

Dear Lord Jesus, we thank You that in the beginning, you were with God the Father and the Holy Spirit in creating the heavens and the earth, and nothing was created apart from you. We thank You, Almighty God, that you are light and that there is no darkness in You. We thank You, Heavenly Father, that You chose to bring us out of the darkness into your glorious light and that You have separated us from the children of darkness.

Thank You, Lord Jesus, that You are the light of the world that shines in the darkness. Thank You, Lord Jesus, that you have revealed yourself to us and that we can walk on the journey of faith with You through this dark world to the promised land of paradise to be with you for all eternity. Lord Jesus, enable us to faithfully follow you wherever You may lead us and for us to declare your mighty acts. Lord Jesus, thank you that You have overcome the world. May we also follow in your footsteps and be victorious in this world. We praise and worship You, Lord Jesus, in your faithfulness and care for us. We pray in Jesus's name, Amen.

Jesus is the light of the world

Bob Dylan has perfectly captured the sign of our times that the choice in life is to either serve the Lord or the devil; there is no other choice or option.[6] So, when we look at the possibilities, we need to know what it means to serve the Lord. So much of current Christian teaching is centred around trying to get the Lord and God to serve us, but that is not an option and only results in endless futility.

Jesus has promised us that whoever follows him will have the light of life and will never walk in darkness (John 8:12). In the argument with the Pharisees that followed, Jesus asserts that He is not of this world and He is from heaven (John 8:23). To follow Jesus, we need to follow in His words and teaching and only then can we be set free from the troubles of this world as we will know the truth and the truth will set us free (John 8:31-33). Anyone who sins is a slave to sin, and we see this in the struggles of life where people are caught in an endless cycle, whether it be with depression, worries about making ends meet, or whether they are caught up with addictions, such as drugs, smoking or alcohol abuse. However, if Jesus sets us free, then we will be free indeed (John 8:36).

---

6   Wikipedia. Gotta Serve Somebody. Bob Dylan. Released August 20, 1979

What does it mean to be followers of Jesus?

To understand what it means to follow Jesus, we need to go back to the basics and start at the beginning. In the beginning, Jesus, in conjunction with God the Father and the Holy Spirit, created all things; nothing exists apart from Jesus (John 1:1-3). When we read through the gospels, we sometimes lose sight of the fact that everything created was created by Jesus and through Jesus. It is important to realise that Jesus was the light that shone in the darkness and that the darkness failed to contain the light. Those who oppose Jesus and claim that Christianity is irrelevant in the 21st century need to take a closer look at who Jesus is. Nothing exists without God's permission, even those who do evil. We, as Christians, are called to love our enemies and pray for those who persecute us, whether that be a neighbour, a parent, a relative, or our bosses at work (Matthew 5:43-44). Why are we called to pray for these people? Because God makes the sun shine on the evil and the righteous, and by praying for our enemies, we become children of our Heavenly Father (Matthew 5:45).

It is Jesus who makes God known to His people (John 1:18). We are called to be imitators of God and to live a life of love toward everyone, even those who have deeply hurt us. Our life should be a sacrifice of love (Ephesians 5:1-3). During the tough times that are occurring in Britain right now, we see the sacrificial love of parents who are going without food so that their children don't go hungry. Other people are going out of their way to help the poor and the needy at some cost to themselves. We witness the selfless love of the National Health Service staff who have put their lives at risk to help those suffering from Covid-19, even to death in many cases.

However, much of what passes for religion has moved away from making sacrifices for God and taking up our crosses to follow Jesus. It has been replaced by a 'God wants to make us rich' heresy. Paul states that greed must not even be mentioned among us, but it is a popular theme among Christian television channels (Ephesians 5:3). Does God want to bless us? Yes, he does. Did Jesus come so that we may have a more abundant life? Yes, of course He did (John 10:10). There is more to life than being rich and having lots of possessions. We are called to store up our treasure in heaven where it cannot rust or tarnish (Matthew 6:19-21). Our hearts will be wherever we store our treasure. In this respect, a popular saying among churchgoers today is, *"Don't be too heavenly-minded that we are of no earthly good."* Nevertheless, what I observe is that many churchgoers today are so earthly-minded they are of no heavenly use. The challenge is to renew our minds and be transformed to focus on the tasks at hand and why we were sent to the earth to deliver the light in the darkness (Romans 12:2). We are to set our minds on the heavenly things above (Colossians 2:2-3).

How should we approach life on earth?

Tozer has stated that we live in a perpetual crisis; sin has been put down, and Christ reigns over a redeemed world.[7] Politicians are striving to bring us back to a state of normality and to bring the economy back on an even footing. Yet while sin abounds in our countries, they are doomed to failure. We may well ask the question,

---

7   A. W. Tozer. Born After Midnight. Chapter 6. We live in a state of emergency, page 28. Christian Publications, Inc. Pennsylvania, USA. 1959.

"What would Jesus do?" To answer that question, we must return to look more closely at the life of Jesus.

Firstly, Jesus aligned himself with sinners when he was baptised by John the Baptist (Matthew 3:13-17). Remember, John was calling people to repent of their sins, turn to God and be baptised into the new life, which is the Life of the Kingdom of God (Matthew 3:1-10). God was pleased with Jesus because He had aligned himself with the sinners of the world. Without being affiliated with the sins of mankind, he could not be the sacrificial lamb who could wash away the sins of the world.

Secondly, Jesus was led by the Holy Spirit into the desert to be tempted by Satan (Matthew 4:1). Jesus had to overcome the ruler of this world, the devil. We are all familiar with the three temptations Jesus faced and His response to overcome the temptations by quoting scripture from Deuteronomy (Matthew 4:3-11). Jesus warned us that in this world, we would face many troubles and persecution, but we were to be encouraged because Jesus has overcome the world (John 16:33). Again, Jesus is aligned and identifies with our situation. We are to pray not to be led into temptation but that we may be delivered from the evil one who is Satan (Matthew 6:13). We are tested every day by things that are common temptations for mankind because God wants to remain central in our lives. He is sufficient for all our daily requirements, and temptations and is there to help us persevere and overcome the world (1 Corinthians 10:13).

Tozer warns us that Satan hates God for no other reason than that God is supreme. As man is created in God's image, Satan's hatred is particularly vicious toward mankind.[8] When we look closely

---

8   A. W. Tozer. Born After Midnight. Chapter 9. What to do about the devil, page 41.

at what is happening in the world, we see that lawlessness is abounding. The challenges of daily living can be related to the fall of man and the abominable hatred of Satan against mankind.

The life of Christ

An unpopular Biblical truth today is that if we want to follow Jesus, we must take the path of the cross (Matthew 16:24-26). Paul E. Billheimer refers to the cross as being the throne of the universe.[9] If we want to be victorious in our lives and experience the increasing power and victory over our selfish lives, and victory over our daily battles with sin, we must come to the realisation that even though we have been born again and filled with the Holy Spirit, we are still fallen people.[10] In John Bunyan's, classic, *The Pilgrim's Progress*, Pilgrim was not delivered from his heavy burden until he came to the foot of the cross.[11] Prosperity is part of the gospel, but the biggest part of the gospel is the sacrificial way of life.[12]

Tenney charts Jesus' life on earth through several stages as recorded and presented in John's gospel.[13] The period of consideration was when Jesus came before the public for their consideration and acceptance (John 1:19-4:54). This was followed by a period of controversy when the claims of Jesus as the Son

---

Christian Publications, Inc. Pennsylvania, USA. 1959.

9   Paul E. Billheimer. Overcomers Through the Cross. Chapter 1. The throne of the universe is a cross. Pages 9-10. Kingsway Publications, Sussex, UK. 1982.

10   IBID, Chapter 2. How to use the cross, page 20.

11   John Bunyan. The Pilgrim's Progress. Part the first, page 35. Banner of Truth, Edinburgh, UK, 1979.

12   Bilheimer, IBID, page 21.

13   Merrill C. Tenney. John: The Gospel of Belief: An Analytical Study of the Text. William B. Eerdmanns Publishing Company, Grand Rapids, USA. 1997

of God, the Jewish Messiah, the Gentile Christ began to become understood by his audiences (John 5:1 – 6:71). Then a period of conflict ensued in which there was a clear hostility to Jesus among the religious leaders, and they decided that Jesus must be killed (John 7:1 – 11:53). John describes a crisis period during which those who believed in Jesus had to consolidate their belief, and the unbelievers found Jesus intolerable (John 11:54 –12:36). There is a period of conference, which Tenney describes as a transition period, where Jesus moves from a public ministry to providing final instructions for believers (John 12:37–16:36). It is salient to consider what claims Jesus made for himself within the Gospel of John.

I am the bread of life (John 6:35)

The promise is that all who come to Jesus will never be hungry, nor will they be thirsty. It is true to say that most of us are looking for a meaning to our lives, and on a spiritual level, we have a deep need to know our place and our purpose. Those who are poor in spirit and realise that they need God in their lives will find a place in God's Kingdom (Matthew 5:3). Those who are hungry and thirsty for God's righteousness will be fulfilled and find contentment in the world (Matthew 5:6). Jesus satisfies the hungry soul with good things (Psalm 109:7). Jesus can deliver us from our distress in times of trouble (Psalm 107:28). King David declared that though he was now old in years that he had never seen the righteous bereft of God or the children of the righteous needing to beg for bread (Psalm 37:25). Even though we may suffer for a little while, ultimately God will bring us through the storm. If we delight in the Lord and focus upon him, he has promised to fulfil the desires of our hearts (Psalm 37:4 - 5). Life is more important than food and clothing. If we focus on seeking God's Kingdom and His righteousness, then all our earthly needs will be met (Matthew 6:25-34). Let's not spend time being anxious about our needs but spend more time in prayer, seeking what God is trying to teach us. We are called to watch and pray so that we may not be found short and miss the purpose of our current challenges (Matthew 26:41). We are called to watch and pray to ensure that we see what is coming ahead of us and not to be weighed down by the troubles of the world (Luke 21:34-36).

We are called not to be troubled by the things that are happening around us but to believe in Jesus as our Saviour and to believe in God as our Father in heaven (John 14:1). Jesus is preparing a place in heaven for each and every person who has called upon his name to be saved from the coming anger and judgement of God. Jesus has left us His peace, so there is no need to be worried or afraid of the future (John 14:27). If we focus on Jesus, then we won't be weighed down by the transient problems in this world. We will be encouraged by the coming eternal life that is promised through faith in Jesus the Messiah (2 Corinthians 4:17-18).

I am the light of the world (John 8:12)

Jesus is the light of the world and offers us a new life through being born again through the water of baptism and through the indwelling of the Holy Spirit in our lives (John 3:5). Without the Holy Spirit, we cannot enter the Kingdom of God. Belief in Jesus takes us out of the darkness of our old life and brings us into His light: His glorious presence (1 Peter 2:9). Before encountering Jesus, we were a people who sat in darkness, and now we have seen a great light (Isaiah 9:2 and Matthew 4:16). We have already seen that God is light and that there is no darkness around God. In heaven, there will be no need for a sun or moon because God's light will shine forth and fill the heavens with His illumination.

The light can illuminate and shine upon what is good and evil and, through the word of God, show us the areas of our life that remain in darkness and need to come into God's light (John 1:9). The light can open our eyes to God's ways and to help transform and renew our minds on heavenly things (Romans 12:1-2). God also requires that we shine as lights to the world, leading those who are lost out of darkness into God's wonderful light (Matthew 5:14-16). The world desperately requires us to be beacons and to illuminate what is right from what is evil.

Light is required for plants to grow; without light, there would be no food chain, the world's ecosystem would collapse, and life on earth would not be viable. Light from the sun is needed to warm the planet, and without light, there would be a barren planet full of ice.[14]

I am the gate for the sheep (John 10:7-9)

The people of God are referred to as sheep and God's own flock in several places in the Bible, and it is worth noting that God is the one who leads His sheep.

While rejoicing at the faithfulness of God, we need to keep in full focus the righteousness of God. When Jesus came to be baptised

---

14   My printable faith. https://myprintablefaith.com/the-7-i-ams-of-jesus/

by John, He came to fulfil the righteousness of God (Matthew 3:15). God's response to Jesus's baptism was to be very pleased and to send down His Spirit on Jesus, which descended as a dove (Matthew 3:16-17). John was baptising those who had repented of their old lives and had changed direction. Firstly, we need to acknowledge that we have gone our own way apart from God and followed our own desires (Isaiah 53:6). This led to God placing all our sins and iniquities on Jesus. The water of baptism is a symbol of our passing from our old life that leads to death into a new life. Jesus's baptism signified that He stood with every sinner. Repentance is the sole foundation upon which everything in the Kingdom of God is to be built.[15] Repentance is something that we must do on a daily basis, for we need to develop a contrite spirit and a heart that totally rejects the way of the world.[16] To come out of darkness into the light of God's truth, there is a need to pray for the light of God, the light of truth, to be continually shed into our lives upon our words and deeds.[17] The biggest obstacle to coming into the light is our own pride and self-righteousness. Those who hunger and thirst after God's righteousness will be filled (Matthew 5:6). We need to seek God's Kingdom and His righteousness above all else (Matthew 6:33). If we are persecuted because we align with Jesus's righteousness, then ours is the Kingdom of Heaven, and we will receive our reward in heaven (Matthew 5:10-12). Our righteousness needs to surpass that of the religious leaders of Jesus's day (Matthew 5:20). Our

---

15   Basilea Schlink. Repentance: The Joy-Filled Life, page 47. Lakeland Marshall Pickering Ltd, Basingstoke, UK. 1985.
16   IBID, page 52.
17   IBID, page 52.

righteousness should not be for show but with a respectful heart toward God (Matthew 6:1). Open our eyes to see in a new light all that Jesus is doing and come to repentance (Matthew 21:32). Remember that God made Jesus, who had no sin, to be sin for us so that we may possess the righteousness of God (2 Corinthians 5:21). The righteousness of the sheep comes through faith in our Lord and Saviour (Philippians 3:9).

I am the good shepherd (John 10:11-15)

If Jesus is the good shepherd, there must exist bad or evil shepherds who aim to lead the sheep away from God. Anyone entering into God's Kingdom via Jesus will be saved. We are safe in Jesus because Jesus keeps us safe. Jesus came so that we may have a life of abundance. The gate that leads to destruction is wide and easy to find, but the narrow gate of Jesus that leads to eternal life is small (Matthew 7:13-14). By following the Lord, we will not lack anything, and our souls will be restored (Psalm 23:1-2). Jesus leads us in the pathways of righteousness, and even if we come close to evil, we have no need to be afraid or worry, for the peace of God, which passes all understanding, will walk beside us. The promise is that God's goodness and mercy will be with us all the days of our life, and God will bring us home to His house forever (Psalm 23:6).

Then the sheep of God's pasture will praise Him forever, and each generation will recount the wonderful acts that God has performed on behalf of his people (Psalm 79:13). God's sheep recognise that He is our creator and that we dwell in His pasture.

Therefore, we should give thanks and see that the Lord's love endures through all generations (Psalm 100:3-4). If we are in Christ, then we are renewed as a new creation; the old has passed, and the new life in Christ has come (2 Corinthians 5:17). Very few actually live as if they are born again and are living the new life that Christ offers. More than ever, believers in the Western world are consumed with the daily challenges of trying to live in an ever-demanding world that is sliding toward its end. However, we should constantly remind ourselves that when Jesus appears at His second coming, we shall be like Him (1 John 3:2).

I am the resurrection and the life (John 11:25)

Jesus is the gateway to eternal life: an everlasting life lived out in the presence of God. The promise is that though we depart from this world, we will never die. Indeed, the Bible frequently refers to those who have passed as "being asleep" while we wait for the resurrection of believers. The grave did not hold Jesus, and those who came looking for Jesus after His crucifixion, could not find Him because He had risen (Mark 16:6; Luke 24:22-27). The resurrection life that is promised to believers in Christ is something that should be looked forward to with expectation and excitement. Born-again believers in Christ have been promised a living hope through the resurrection of Jesus and through the mercy of God (1 Peter 1:3). The water of baptism promises us a clean conscience through the resurrection of Jesus so that in all things, Jesus remains the only gate to salvation and eternal life (1 Peter 3:21). We wait patiently for the coming of the

Lord and the archangel who with a loud trumpet call will hasten us to be with God forever (1 Thessalonians 4:14-17). Therefore, worthy is Jesus, who was slain for our sins to receive the glory, the power of God, all wisdom and the praise and worship of all of us who have been saved (Revelation 5:12-13).

I am the way, the truth, and the life (John 14:6)

It is true to say that, at the name of Jesus, every knee will bow, on the earth, under the earth and above the earth, and every tongue will confess that Jesus Christ is Lord to the glory of God the Father (Philippians 2:9-12). Those who reject Jesus in this life will come face-to-face with him before God's throne. All creation will acknowledge and confess that Jesus is Lord of Lords and King of Kings, either willingly because they are the redeemed of the Lord or unwillingly, having rejected Jesus while living on the earth.

Jesus is the image of the invisible Father, the Almighty God, the God who sits upon the throne of heaven (Colossians 1:15). Anyone who has seen Jesus has seen the Father: the two are both distinct but the same (John 14:9). All of us who have a vision of Jesus and are led by him have already seen the Father who is in heaven. Jesus is the radiance of Almighty God's glory and the exact image of the living God. Everything has its being through the power of Jesus's mighty word. Once Jesus had completed salvation for all who believe, He now sits at the right hand of God (Hebrews 1:3). Those who believe will experience that Jesus has all the treasures and knowledge required to live our lives in faith (Colossians 2:2-

3). In these dark times, we need to become a people of vision and imitators of our Lord, and to be rooted and built up through our faith in Jesus (Colossians 2:7).

Jesus has promised that everyone who embraces His teaching and commandments will know the truth, and the truth will set them free (John 8:31-32). The exciting part of this vision from Christ is that the Bible teaches that we are seen as already being raised with Christ. Therefore, it is all the more reason to set our minds on the things that await us in heaven (Colossians 3:1-2).

We are called to put to death everything that is in our worldly nature, including sexual immorality, which is an ever-increasing problem in these last days we live in (Colossians 3:5). All impurities, lust after the things of the world, such as earthly position or possessions. Put away all evil desires, jealousy, greed and idolatry: anything we place a higher value upon over and above God. There is a second list of common human traits that we are commanded to rid ourselves of, including anger, rage, being malicious, slandering others, lying to each other and all swearing (Colossians 3:8). Therefore, the Bible leaves us in no doubt as to what must be removed from our lives. It is clear that without continually submitting to the Lord in repentance and asking for supernatural help, we have no way of overcoming these worldly desires of a sinful nature.

The Bible also provides a model for what we should replace our earthly desires with, including compassion, kindness, humility, gentleness, patience, forgiveness, and to love our fellow humans with the love of God (Colossians 3:12-15). Giving thanks and praise is a major part of our living as Christians, as is allowing the word of God to change us and bring us out of darkness into His wonderful light.

I am the true vine (John 15:1)

The key message is remaining connected to Jesus, and in order to achieve this, we should regularly reflect on the teaching and commandments that Jesus gave us. If we love Jesus, then we must obey Jesus's commands and teaching (John 14:21-23). The purpose of remaining in Jesus is that it is the only way to bear fruit that is heavenly and not burnt up in the furnace that will test all our works. The hindrances to abiding and growing in Christ are explained in the Parable of the Sower (Matthew 13:1-23). The seed, which is the word of God, depends on where the seed is sown. The seed scattered on the path is stolen by the evil one, and the seed sown on rocky places is unable to develop roots, so it is dissipated. When the word is sown among thorns, then the worries of this world cause the word to shrivel and die. The worries of the world, especially with high fuel bills and soaring food costs, are an indication of the times and a reason why there are not so many people coming to Christ in the Western countries who are afflicted at the moment. The key to abiding in Christ is to ensure that our hearts are filled with good soil. This allows the word of God to grow within us so that we may bear a solid crop that yields much more than was sown in our hearts.

If we remain in Christ, then the promise is that we may ask whatever we wish in accordance with God's will, and it shall be given to us (John 15:7). It is to the glory of God that his children bear much fruit to help grow the Kingdom of God. The good news is that we did not choose Jesus, but He chose us. It is His desire that we go and bear fruit for the Kingdom of God (John 15:16). Therefore, God, who began the good work of making us holy because he is holy, will carry it on to completion until the day of the Lord's return (Philippians 1:6).

Prayer

Dear Lord Jesus, thank You that you have promised us the light that leads to eternal life. Praise You, Lord Jesus. As a believer in You as my Lord and Saviour, I now walk in Your eternal light, and I no longer fear the darkness. Praise You, Lord Jesus, that anyone who has seen You has also seen our Heavenly Father, Almighty and everlasting God. We praise You, Lord, that You are the bread of life and that everyone who comes to You will never go away hungry or thirsty. Lord Jesus, we acknowledge that You are the narrow door that leads to eternal life. There is no other way by which mankind be saved from the coming anger of God, who has to judge the sins and rebellion of the world. Dear Lord Jesus, You are the good shepherd who leads Your sheep and followers beside still water and sees that we lack no good thing. Praise You, Lord, that you are the resurrection, the life and the gateway to paradise. You are the way, the truth and the life. Teach me to walk in Your light in these dark days of the end of this age. You, Lord Jesus, are the true vine and help me, Lord, to stay grafted in You so that I may produce much fruit for your Kingdom. In Jesus's name, we pray. Amen.

God so loved the world

*For God so loved the world that he gave His
one and only Son, that whoever believes in him
shall not perish but have eternal life.*

(John 3:16, New International Version)

None of us needs any introduction to this verse; it is one of the most popular and familiar, if not the most popular. We all want to be loved, but few of us ever attain the kind of love we crave, the love that brings contentment, security and, above all else, safety. A love that will reach down deep within us to heal our deepest hurts and move those profound insecurities that we all have and seem extensively embedded in our souls. Yet that is the immeasurable love that God offers us, and it is ours to possess freely if we only accept it. All of us are born with fathomlesslongings and needs. From our earliest memories to the day we die, we seek and crave fulfilment. We seek fulfilment in many areas, in our careers, our families, our hobbies, and with our friends. However, there is truly only one place to receive the love we long for, and that is in Christ. The problem lies in our ability to receive that perfect love from God.

Our relationship with our earthly parents will fashion, to a greater or lesser extent, our ability to receive love from our Heavenly Father, and there lies most of our problems. We question if God truly loves us and if he really cares about us. This is particularly true if we have a bad or poor relationship with our earthly father. Our image of God is moulded by our relationship with our earthly father; it is natural to compare our relationship with our parents with that of Almighty God. Even if we do not do it consciously, we are bound to do it unconsciously. It is becoming more common for children to have poor relationships with their parents, particularly in the Western world with its high divorce rates. It is possible that our parents have abandoned us to pursue life elsewhere. For many, we were abused by our parents either physically or emotionally, and that has left deep scars that require healing. Among the scars are questions for God. *"If you love me so much, why did you allow this to happen to me? Where were you when I needed you the most? Why didn't you help me during my trauma or my torture?"* The answer, of course, is that God was exactly where He was when His Son was being crucified for our sins. That sounds a little glib, but it's the truth, and it is an important part of the jigsaw that is life as we experience it.

God saw from the beginning what man required and craved, for He created us. Some of that creation of mankind was to manufacture withi our being a huge part of us that can only find fulfilment in God. Once we fell from grace in the Garden of Eden, God began to implement His plan in His time. God knew that redeeming mankind would cost Him everything. He gave His most precious thing - the one thing He could not bear to be separated from - so that you and I could be reconciled to Him. God took the initiative to reach out to us in love. It was a costly love; the price was everything that God had to give. Jesus said, 'I and the Father are one. Whoever has seen me has seen the Father.' The significance of these statements is that not only is Jesus equal to God, but he is, in every sense, God. Mankind put God to death on a cross, and the death was both agonising and cursed. It was the only time in history that Jesus was separated from the Father. It was a terrible price to pay for the redemption of mankind and should be sufficient that we never call God's love into question. He loved us with an everlasting love. God died for our sins so that we might be reconciled and reunited with Him. The question is whether or not we will accept His love and if we will receive all that He has planned for us.

God loved us. We were lost, without hope, dead in our transgressions and destined for eternal damnation, but God loved us so much that He found the solution to our problem. He took our place. 'Let me take all that you deserve so that you may go free.' No greater love has any man that he would lay down his life for a friend, yet God laid down his life for His enemies. While we were still sinners, God died for us. He replaced our sins with the perfect life of His Son. Jesus sacrificed himself so that we may go free.

Accepting Jesus

The truth is that whosoever receives and accepts Jesus as Lord and Saviour has the right to join God's family. That is the good news of salvation. It is God's desire that no man perishes, but all come to salvation and eternal life. The difficult part is accepting that love and bowing down before Him in recognition that there is no other way that a man can be saved but through the sacrifice of Jesus Christ on the cross. God so loved us that He gave us the freedom to choose between eternal life and eternal damnation; the choice is ours. There is a deep longing in us to be loved for who we are, to be loved unconditionally without fear of losing that love by some action or decision on our part. God has loved us with an everlasting love, and He will continue to love us with an everlasting love. God's love is pure and is not dependent on anything we do. He is there for us; He has promised never to leave or forsake us. Even to the end of the age, God is there with us, beside us. When we hurt, He hurts; when we rejoice, He rejoices. That is the wonder of God's love for mankind. Each one of us is precious in his sight; He knows everything there is to know about us. He knows our weaknesses and our strengths. He knows our thoughts, the good and the bad ones. He knows when we lie down and when we get up. Whatever we do is visible to God; whatever we think is visible to God. Our hearts may deceive us, but God knows the incentives behind our actions. We may deceive ourselves and not want to face up to what we are really doing, yet God knows the motif, and He still loves us. Even when we are at our most wicked, God loves us.

Receiving God's love

The question is, how can we know that love? The answer is by allowing God in and not blocking Him out. We need to come to that point where we accept God's love, and that may not be easy if we have deep hurt within us. The good news is that God reaches us where we are. He accepts us as we are with the emotional baggage we carry around with us. However, God loves us too much to leave us that way. If we let Him into our lives and into our hearts, then God will begin to change us. The decision to accept Jesus as Lord and Saviour is life-changing and marks the beginning, not the end, of our journey with God - a journey that will ultimately lead to eternal life.

When we accept Jesus as Lord and Saviour, we pass from death to life. While God loves us as we are, He loves us too much to leave us that way. There are things in our lives that, at best, are unhealthy and, at worst, are wicked and evil. God will begin to bring them to the forefront to be dealt with and removed. His purpose is to make us more like His Son, to be made perfect. For some, that may seem like a catch, but the truth is that God wants us to be Holy as He is Holy. A rough definition of holy is to be dedicated to God, to be God-centred and wish to be like His Son. To be like Christ and to be Christ-like, our lives should reflect something of Jesus. The practical outworking of that objective and goal is that once we accept Jesus as Lord and enter the Kingdom of God, our desires change. When God looks at us, He wants to see Jesus looking back at Him. Our purpose in the world is to be ambassadors for God. Rather than chasing after the things of this world, our purpose, energy and objectives need to be centred on furthering the Kingdom of God. What are we doing that enables the Kingdom of God to grow on the earth? What is our testimony of Christ, and what is there in us that would attract a non-believer to desire what we have?

The answer to that question should be the love and peace we find in our daily relationship with Jesus. For us to grow as Christians, we have to spend quality time with God to enable our relationship with God to develop. Our time with God should not be one-way, a time we continually pray and request or even demand blessings, but should include studying his word in order to understand what it means to be part of the Kingdom of God. It should also include a time of listening for His instructions to us which are vital if we are to follow Him. As the darkness of these last days continues to grow, we need more than at any other time in the history of the world to have a spiritual direction to follow. That will only come about as we learn to listen to what God is saying to us, both as a collective people of God, the body of His church, and as individuals. We need to seek a clear answer to the question, *"In what direction is God taking me - Where does the Lord want me to be?"* To get an answer, we first obviously have to ask the Lord, and second, we have to be in a position to both hear the answer and to test that we have heard correctly.

Rejecting God's provision

A popular saying in today's Western world is that people prefer the God of the New Testament to the God of the Old Testament. However, we are told that God is the same, yesterday and forever (Hebrews 13:8, Revelation 4:8). Modern societies want to believe that God will not bring judgement on the world and will not send anyone to hell; that is not what the Bible teaches. Anyone who believes in Jesus has eternal life, but anyone who rejects Jesus will not see life because God's anger remains upon him (John 3:36). Don't be deceived; the unrighteous will not enter the Kingdom of God (1 Corinthians 6:9-11, see also Matthew 13:49-50, 22:13, 25:30, 25:46, Luke 13:1-5, Luke

16:20-24). Men preferred darkness rather than the light (John 3:19). When the anger of God is poured out on the world, Kings, the mighty and every man and woman who is not of Christ will hide in caves and mountains to escape the anger of God (Revelation 6:15-17).

Prayer

Almighty God and our dear Heavenly Father, we are so grateful that Jesus came into the world so that our sins may be forgiven. We praise and rejoice in You that you have provided a way for believers in Jesus to pass over from the darkness into Your wonderful light. We continually repent of our old lives and pray that You will complete the work You have started in us so that we may be counted among the righteous. Dear Father, may we never presume that we are righteous or take for granted the wonderful gift of eternal life, but rather continue each day to walk in Your ways and follow the teaching and commands of our Lord and Saviour Jesus. Thank you, Father, that we may come boldly to ask for forgiveness and blessing in our time of need knowing that you hear us and we can depend on Your favour through Jesus Christ our Lord. In Jesus's name, we pray, Amen.

The miracles of Jesus

C. S. Lewis defined a miracle 'as an interference with nature by a supernatural power.'[18] We could add that a miracle is an action that defies the laws of science, thus making it a supernatural phenomenon. During his earthly ministry, Jesus performed or carried out 35 miracles that were recorded in the gospels, which affected a number of spheres.[19] Ryrie identifies four Greek words that the gospels use to describe a miracle. *Dunamis* describes the mighty power of God that is displayed in the miracle, *teras* means wonder and highlights the extraordinary nature of the miracle, *ergon* which is commonly translated as works in English, and *semeion*, which means a sign and shows that the miracle was not for show but to instruct us of a spiritual truth.[20]

Seven signs and wonders recorded in John's gospel

The first sign: Jesus changing water into wine at a wedding in Cana is considered by most scholars to be the first miracle that Jesus performed. The miracle showed that Jesus had come to provide a

---

18 C.S. Lewis. Miracles, page 5. Harper Collins Publishers, London, UK, 2012 edition.
19 Charles C. Ryrie. The Miracles of Our Lord, page 11. Loizeaux Brothers, New Jersey, USA, 1988 edition.
20 IBID, page 10.

quality to life (John 2:1-11).[21] It also showed that Jesus was different and could be set apart from ordinary people. It illustrated that Jesus had power over creation and reminds us of the beginning of John's gospel: that Jesus was there in the beginning and nothing was created apart from Jesus.[22] Wine is regarded as an emblem or trademark of the joy life can bring (Psalm 16:11; Psalm 104:15).[23]

The second sign: The second sign recorded in John's gospel is the healing of the nobleman's son (John 4:43-54). This miracle shows that distance was no barrier to Jesus's ability to heal as the nobleman's son was healed at a distance of over 20 miles from where Jesus proclaimed the healing.[24] However, the miracle led Jesus to proclaim that unless the people around him saw a miracle they would not believe (John 4:48). This reminds us of the fact that we cannot please God without faith. The disciple Thomas believed in Jesus's resurrection because he saw Jesus standing before him; therefore, his faith was based upon his eyewitness account. However, Jesus is more impressed by those who believe in him without seeing him or witnessing a miracle (John 20:29). It is good to know that distance is not an issue when we seek answers to our prayers. Also, there are no restrictions on the distance when seeking God's intervention in our personal circumstances. The outcome of the healing of the nobleman's son is that the official's whole household believed in Jesus and that the faith of the household was increased.

---

21 Merrill C. Tenney. John: The Gospel of Belief, page 312. William B Eerdmans Publishing Company, Michigan, USA. 1997 edition.
22 Ryrie, IBID, pages 15-16.
23 Ryrie, IBID, page 16.
24 Tenney, IBID, page 30.

The third sign: The third sign of Jesus's unique power is the healing at the Bethesda pool, which shows Jesus's dominance over time.[25] The man had been ill for 38 years, and there is a clear indication that the man had given up all hope of ever being healed. However, if there was anything positive about the man, then it was in the fact that he had persisted for such a long time. There was always a hope or possibility of God healing him.[26] It is also noteworthy that Jesus sought the man out to warn him not to continue sinning, or a worse fate could become him. This fits in with the thinking of the time: that illness was associated with a sinful life, as can be seen by the disciples' question to Jesus regarding the man born blind (John 9:2). It is important to keep in mind God's purposes and not to assume that we know all the answers behind the circumstances of individual lives. Nevertheless, Jesus has authority over disease, illness and afflictions. It is pertinent to enquire, as Jesus did, whether a person would like to be healed (John 5:6). The man simply had to respond to Jesus's command to pick up his mat and walk (John 5:8). Sometimes the simplest commands from our Lord can prove the most difficult to carry out. In the case of the man at the pool, there was no hesitation. He immediately picked up his mat and walked without pain or any kind of hindrance.

In life, there are those who are envious of what the Lord is doing. In the case of this miracle, the Jews were put out because it occurred on the Sabbath day. The man was carrying his mat on the Sabbath, which was considered by the Jews as work and was

---

25 Tenney, IBID, page 31.
26 Tenney, IBID, pages 104-105.

prohibited under their interpretation of the law. As Jesus pointed out, the Sabbath was made for man, not the opposite (Mark 2:27). We must be very careful and prayerful to ensure that our religious or theological preferences and interpretations of the scriptures do not interfere with or hinder the work of the Lord or the move of the Holy Spirit. Jesus's biggest battles during his time in the world were against the religious leaders of his day.

The fourth sign: Particular consideration must be given to the fourth sign in John's gospel, the feeding of the five thousand, because it is the only miracle recorded in all four gospels. Therefore, we can consider that it was the most important miracle performed by Jesus during his time on the earth (John 6:1-15). Firstly, Jesus's disciples could not feed the great crowd because feeding such a large group is beyond the natural resources of man. The multiplication of sufficient food to feed such a large crowd from five loaves and two fishes shows Jesus's authority over quantity.[27] Furthermore, not only did Jesus multiply the food to feed this huge crowd, but there was plenty over. The message is that God provides abundant food for everyone. However, in the world today, half the world has a surplus of food, and we refer to food mountains, while the other half of the world lives in poverty and in fear of famines. It has been stated that half of the world is on a constant diet trying to lose weight while the other half is slowly starving. Food has to be distributed better across the world. As previously stated, King David was able to say that he was once young, but now he was old. Still, he had never experienced the righteous abandoned or the children of the righteous needing

---

27   Tenney, IBID, page 31.

to beg for food (Psalm 37:25). God provides an abundance of food for the people of Jerusalem who were starving because they were under siege by their enemies (see 2 Kings 7). The guard, who did not believe that God could provide even if the floodgates of heaven were opened, was the person who did not partake in God's provision. The good shepherd satisfies and looks after the needs of his sheep and points back to Jesus being the bread of life (John 6:25-35).

The fifth sign: The fifth sign in John's gospel is Jesus's walking on water (John 6:16-24). The miracle shows that Jesus had power over nature and shows the heresy of Liberal theologians that do not believe in miracles that occur outside of the laws of science.[28] Unbelief is a terrible thing in the eyes of the Lord. It is recorded in Matthew's account that Jesus sent the disciples on ahead of him in the boat while he went into the mountainside to pray (Matthew 14:22-23).

When carrying out the Lord's work, the disciples were buffeted and struggled against the wind, and we can expect similar opposition when we carry out the Lord's instructions. We have been warned that we struggle against rulers, authorities, and the spiritual forces of darkness in the heavenly realms who stand against the purposes of God (Ephesians 6:12). Prayer is important when encountering the unknown in the spiritual life because we need to see clearly and understand when we face the miraculous in the spiritual world. The disciples were initially afraid of what they saw until Jesus reassured them that it was he who was coming to meet them in their struggle (Matthew 14:26-27). Keeping our eyes upon Jesus is essential when

---

28   Tenney, IBID, page 115.

walking in the spiritual realm, lest we sink and drown as Peter was about to when he took his eyes off Jesus (Matthew 14:30-31). Are we prepared to get out of the relative safety of the boat? It appears from this account that the majority of the disciples preferred to stay in the boat. Finally, it was only when Jesus got into the boat alongside the disciples that the storm died down. The outcome of the miracle that the disciples witnessed led to their recognition of Jesus as the Son of God (Matthew 14:32-33).

The sixth sign: The sixth sign in John's gospel is the healing of the man born blind (John 9:1-12). It shows that Jesus had dominion over misfortune.[29] The popular opinion of the disciples' day is that the man who was bought blind was under the judgement of God for some undeclared sin, either caused by his parents or somehow by the man himself (John 9:2). It is certainly true that misfortune in the world today is due to the fall of man from the Garden of Eden. Yet it is untrue that individual misfortune is necessarily due to an individual's sin or the sins of a parent. However, God has promised in the Ten Commandments that He will punish the children for the idolatry of their fathers to the third or fourth generation (Deuteronomy 5:8-9, Numbers 14:18). Furthermore, the man who was healed by the pool was warned not to keep on sinning because something worse might happen to him. It is also true that God punishes the sins of a nation, even though He is patient and hopes that a nation may turn from its wicked and evil ways (Genesis 15:12-16). Israel and Judah were sent into exile for their sins against the Lord and for not keeping God's decrees and commandments (2 Kings 17:12-20).

---

29   Tenney, IBID, page 31.

The man born blind offers an opportunity for the work of God to be displayed in the man's life. The reason for his blindness is not that the man should suffer for half of his life and be reduced to begging so that God could come along and heal him. It is more likely that Jesus is able to use the man's situation so that the work of God can be seen by all. Jesus reemphasises that He is the light of the world, and He has come to bring light to those who are in darkness.

How do we interpret the miracles of God? No one disputes that the man born blind has been healed, but the question remains: by what means has the man been healed? Is his healing an act of God or an act of sorcery? Where we stand when we witness the movement of God in our lives, our churches, our country or in the world, in general, will say a lot about our understanding of what God is doing in our day and our generation. Will we speak out in support of God, or will we shrink back and hide or pass the buck because we are afraid of what people think (John 9:22-23)? Where do we stand in this story of the man who was born blind but can now see? Are we sceptical that God could do miracles in our generation? Do we not believe the miracle at all because it was performed in a way that does not meet our Biblical stance on how miracles should be performed (John 9:16)? Or do we rejoice because we have been privileged enough to see God moving in our generation? Spiritual blindness may be a symptom of our generation. We cannot see that God is working among us. We may become the generation who could see, but we have become spiritually blind (John 9:39). The man who was healed had no doubt that God had healed him and believed that Jesus is his Saviour (John 9:38). Jesus is the same yesterday, today and forever (Hebrews 13:8). Be very careful that we are not led astray and test the spirits and do not attribute the working of the Holy Spirit to another.

The seventh sign: The raising of Lazarus from the dead shows that Jesus has mastery over death and that death no longer has its sting.[30] The raising of Lazarus is not the only time that Jesus is recorded as raising someone from the dead. Jesus raised a young girl from the dead in Matthew 9:18-26 and also a young man, as recorded in Luke 7:11-17, so the raising of Lazarus was the third time that Jesus raised someone from the dead (John 11:1-44).

Jairus was a leader of his local church and, unlike many church leaders of his day, believed that Jesus could heal his daughter. As parents, we are willing to do anything to help our children have a life that we could only dream of. Yet have we ever come to a point where we question why God is not answering our prayers and why there is a delay? Both the stories of Jairus's daughter and the raising of Lazarus go some way to answering the question of why sometimes our prayers don't bring instantaneous answers.

When Jairus pleaded with Jesus to go with him to heal his daughter, Jesus went immediately without hesitation. Why didn't Jesus just say the word and heal the little girl from a distance? He was certainly capable of healing from a distance. The answer lies in the fact that Jesus could only do what God led him to do, and, in this instance, God had a larger plan. Sometimes the delay is to test our faith because, without faith, it is impossible to please God (Hebrews 11:6). Growing our faith in Christ enables us to grow up to the fullness

---

30   Tenney, IBID, page 31.

of God (Ephesians 3:16-19). Maybe there is a delay in the answer to our prayers because Jesus wants to teach more about healing. Jairus witnessed this during the healing of the sick woman who had spent all her wealth on doctors who could not heal her (Mark 5:25-26). This woman had something that only Jairus possessed among a great crowd of people following Jesus: faith. It was important for the woman and the crowd that Jesus took time to stop and affirm her healing. It was a testimony to the crowd of the power of God and an affirmation that God had honoured her faith (Mark 5:33-34). After 12 years of suffering, the woman was set free to go in peace.

How do we react when we receive bad news? Do we go on believing in Jesus, or do we simply give up and become fatalistic, assuming it was not God's will to answer our prayers? An alternative response is to become bitter at God and assume that God simply doesn't care about us or love us. The response that God is looking for is that we keep on believing in him and ignore the circumstances that are a hindrance to faith (Mark 5:36).

Death is an inevitable consequence of life for most people unless the Messiah returns. Jesus came to deliver us from the fear of death (Hebrews 2:15). Through Christ, death has lost its sting, and Jesus has led us into victory over death (1 Corinthians 15:55-57). Our belief and hope are that we will have eternal life through the atonement that Christ has provided for us through his death on the cross. In raising the widow's son from death, Jesus not only shows his power over death but also his compassion for the widow who had lost her only son (Luke 7:13). Inevitably, Jesus was heralded as a great prophet, and his reputation spread throughout the land.

The purpose of Lazarus's sickness was to bring glory to Jesus. Right from the time that Jesus was informed about the sickness, He knew that it would not ultimately end in death (John 11:4). On hearing that Lazarus was ill, Jesus remained where he was for two more days, while the human response would be to rush to the aid of the person who was ill. This is an example that human thoughts are not the same as God's thoughts, nor are our ways the same as God's ways (Isaiah 55:8-9). God always achieves His purposes, and His timing is perfect. Even though we cannot always see the wider picture of what God is doing, God is always working for our good (Isaiah 55:11-12). Jesus knew that going to Bethany would put him in danger and that Lazarus had fallen asleep (died), but it was time for him to go, so he set out for Bethany (John 11:9-10).

Jesus came to show Israel that he was the resurrection and the life, the promised Messiah (John 11:25-26). As the story unfolds, we see that these are real people with real responses and concerns. The disciples are sure they will be killed if they go to Bethany with Jesus, but they still go with Jesus. Mary understood there would be a resurrection on the last day, but her vision was of the future, not the present. The Jews who knew that Jesus had healed the blind man questioned whether Jesus could have prevented the death of Lazarus. However, their thinking did not extend to seeing the impossible that Jesus could raise Lazarus from the dead. Jesus raised Lazarus to bring glory to himself and God but also to show the people who he really was. How do we respond to seeing miracles? Many of the Jews put their faith in him (John 11:45). The Pharisees and religious leaders responded by acknowledging that Jesus had performed miracles. So, to protect their own interests, they plotted to put Jesus to death (John 11:47-51). The greatest miracle of all was that Jesus died and was raised from death so that all who believe in him shall not perish but have eternal life.

Jesus's miracles carried out on the Sabbath

There are seven miracles recorded in the gospels where Jesus performed a miracle on the Sabbath, the Jewish day of rest.

1. Jesus healed a man with an evil spirit and showed that the evil spirits knew who Jesus was and that Jesus had authority over the spirit world (Mark 1:21-28).

2. Jesus healed Peter's mother-in-law, who had a fever, which in an era when there were no antibiotics, such fevers could lead to death. Jesus has authority over infectious diseases (Mark 1:29-31).

3. Jesus healed a man with a shrivelled hand to show that he has authority over infirmities (Mark 3:1-6). Jesus also demonstrates that it is lawful to do good on the Sabbath (Mark 3:4). It also shows that Jesus is distressed at the hardness of the human heart (Mark 3:5). This miracle also demonstrates the incorrect thinking of the Jews. They were so fixated on not working on the Sabbath that they missed the wider picture: God always works for good; the Sabbath was made for man, and Jesus was Lord of the Sabbath (Mark 2:27-28).

4. As already discussed, Jesus healed the lame man at the pool at Bethesda (John 5:1-18).

5. Jesus healed the man born blind (John 9:1-7).

6. Jesus healed a crippled woman who was bent over by a spirit for 18 years. The leader of the synagogue showed how entrenched religious opinion can be when he angrily told his congregation to come and be healed on any day other than the Sabbath (Luke 13:10-14). Jesus was angered by the hypocrisy of the people who did not value the healing of the woman above their own farm animals (Luke 13:15-16). The miracle also shows that Jesus has dominion over Satan and the evil realm.

7. Jesus healed a man with dropsy when Jesus was having a meal with a prominent religious leader (Luke 14:1-6). The religious experts had no answer to what Jesus was doing or to the questions he was asking them.

Jesus healed diseases and cast out demons

There are many instances in the gospels where Jesus healed all the peoples' diseases and cast out demons from afflicted people (Matthew 8:16, Mark 1:34 and 1:39, Luke 4:41, 6:17-18 and Luke 7:21). These miracles remind us that we live in a world of good and evil where the spiritual world is very real. One man who was healed by Jesus had a legion of demons inside of him, and this gave the man supernatural strength (Luke 8:26-39). The demons feared that Jesus had come to torture them (Luke 8:28). Jesus drove the demons out with a word, and they entered a herd of pigs who rushed into the lake and were drowned (Luke 8:33). The people feared the power of Jesus, and I wonder how we would react to witnessing such a powerful miracle? Jesus had to leave the region but left the man delivered of demons behind to witness on the Lord's behalf.

For the final word on miracles, like the gospels, I have selected only a few to demonstrate the greater purpose of Jesus, who came to provide abundant life for all those who believe. How we react to the signs and miracles around us or our reaction to new movements of the Holy Spirit in our life, the life of our church, community, or the world in general will define who we are and how we have come with our faith. All things are possible with God (Matthew 19:26).

𝔓rayer

Dear Heavenly Father, we are so thankful that You are in control of the cosmos, the universe, the earth and everything in it. We are grateful for Your mercy and Your compassion. We worship and praise you for being the light of the world, the bread of life, the good shepherd, the door for your sheep, the resurrection and the life, the way, the truth and the life, and the true vine. We put our faith and trust in You, Lord Jesus, knowing that we will never go thirsty or hungry because You are the Lord of our lives. We praise you that You are master over space and distance, master over time, master over the quantity of life, and You have dominion over nature and the natural world. We thank you that You have control over our misfortunes, and at the end of life, it is comforting to know that You have mastered death and we can look forward to being resurrected into eternal life. Lord, we worship You, knowing that, with You, all things are possible. Thank you, Lord Jesus, Amen.

Conflicts and parables

There is no doubt that wherever Jesus went, he evoked a strong response, and people either believed in him or rejected him. The responses that Jesus elicited in people reflect the battle between light and darkness and the war between good and evil. How Jesus responded to opposition and his teaching through parables is important in enabling us to see what the Christian life should be in this fallen world. They empower us to respond to what we are called to do in these last days of the late great planet earth.

The period of conflict

Tenney outlines the period of conflict between Jesus and the Jewish authorities as described in John's gospel (7:1 – 11:53).[31] I am only going to refer to two episodes here that point to prejudice and the consequent conflict, as the others have already been covered elsewhere.

Feast of Tabernacles

The Feast of Tabernacles (Sukkot) is one of three major festivals in Israel in which pilgrims travel to the Temple in Jerusalem.[32] The feast

---

31 Tenney, IBID, Chapter 6. The period of conflict, pages 129-180.

32 HTTPS:// www.gotquestions.org/Feast-of-Tabernacles.html

commemorates the 40 years that Israel spent in the wilderness. It begins on the 15th day of the month of Tishri (September or October): five days after the Day of Atonement and at the end of the harvest. It was during this feast that Solomon's Temple was dedicated to God (1 Kings 8:2).

Jesus arrived at the halfway point of the feast, and the Jews were amazed at his teaching. Jesus proclaims that his teaching comes from God the Father and can be verified by anyone who chooses to do God's will (John 7:16). The Jewish religious leaders tried to seize Jesus because of who he was claiming to be and the miracles he was performing. Many of the Jewish crowd put their faith in Jesus, and the authorities sent guards to arrest him, but they were unsuccessful. The conflict was mainly in the hearts of those who heard his teaching. Some believed because of the miracles he was able to perform. Some were confused because they thought he was from Galilee without realising that Jesus was, in fact, born in Bethlehem as prophesied (Micah 5:2). Jesus divided peoples' opinions of who he was, and throughout history, Jesus has continued to divide people as to who he is. After Jesus is glorified, he promises to give the Holy Spirit to anyone who believes in him (John 7:38-39).

The Jewish leaders rejected Jesus because they believed he came from Galilee, and they were too prejudiced to research Jesus's origins (John 7:47-52). The main point for us is to ensure that we carefully examine all aspects of new teaching we may receive and to test the spirits to ensure they are from God.

The woman caught in adultery

The account of the woman caught in adultery is not considered by many scholars to be part of the original gospel. However, the story is full of hypocrisy because the first thing that is missing is where the man is, as it takes two to commit adultery (John 7:53-8:11). The episode appears a deliberate plot by the Pharisees and teachers of the law to trap Jesus.[33] The law demands that people committing adultery are put to death (Leviticus 20:10, Deuteronomy 22:22), which makes the absence of the man even more conspicuous. The Pharisees and teachers of the law are hoping that Jesus would either break the Jewish law by letting the woman go or break the Roman law, which does not permit the Jews to put anyone to death. Jesus took his time to answer them and suggested that the person who was blameless and without sin should be the one to cast the first stone (John 8:7). After hearing Jesus's response, the accusers, who were likely to be all men, began to leave with the older men leaving first. After the men had left, there was no one to condemn the woman. Neither did Jesus condemn her, but instructed her to leave her life of sin (John 8:11).

Jesus forgave the woman for her adultery and was not judgemental of the fact that she had broken one of the ten commandments. Indeed, King David was also forgiven by God for his act of adultery with Bathsheba. This is not to say that committing adultery is not serious in God's eyes, but there is a road to repentance and forgiveness in the Kingdom of God. The story underlines that we should not be so quick to judge other people's sins (Matthew 7:4-5). It also shows us to take time to think when we are explaining the

---

33   Tenney, IBID, Chapter 6. The period of conflict, page 139.

gospel and are confronted by those who are aggressively against the word of God (Acts 6:9-10). The Holy Spirit has promised to guide us into all truth (John 16:13); therefore, we need to be afraid of what we may face in the future. As someone who hates confrontation, the calm way that Jesus handled the aggressive nature of the Pharisees and the teachers of the law is a great role model for us all.

Children of the light or children of the darkness

When we think about who we are, what do we see? Are we confident that we are children of the light and that God has accepted us into his Kingdom because we believe in Jesus? Do we lack confidence, have a poor self-image and struggle with our self-worth? Maybe when we were growing up, people abused us, bullied us or constantly told us that we would never amount to much. Take heart because, in Christ, we are a new creation. In Christ, our old self has passed away, and God is doing new things in our lives (2 Corinthians 5:17). We need to remind ourselves that we are fallen people in a fallen world. We also need to remind ourselves that we are a work in progress. If we have failed in some way today, rather than beating ourselves up, we should look forward to tomorrow, which is another opportunity to put things right. We should try to look at ourselves as God sees us. We are royalty, holy, God's own possession and people of the light (1 Peter 2:9). God loved us with enormous love. Even though we were dead in sin, God made us alive in Christ (Ephesians 2:4-5). We are God's treasured possession (Deuteronomy 7:6, Deuteronomy 26:18, Exodus 19.5). We should keep reminding ourselves that He who began a good work in us will carry it on to completion. God has not given up on us (Philippians 1:6).

In following Jesus, we should continually fix our eyes upon the Lord and be careful to hold to His teaching. Then we will know the truth, and the truth will set us free (John 8:32). If Jesus sets us free from whatever barriers there are in our lives, then we shall be free to move forward in our lives (John 8:36).

However, we must be careful not to fall into the errors of the Jews who assumed that because they were descended from Abraham that they were accepted by God (John 8:33). Similar errors can occur in our day; for example, if we think because we go to church every Sunday and attend prayer meetings regularly, we are saved. Or, if we believe in God, that is enough to be saved; it is not. We have to be followers and disciples of Jesus and keep to His teaching to enter the Kingdom of God. We need to continually repent of the sin in our lives and ensure that we remain humble and contrite in our hearts. Pride is an insidious sin that can blind us to who we really are, especially when we begin to consider ourselves better than others. The sin of the Pharisees was that they considered themselves better than other people and were not like tax collectors, robbers, evildoers, or adulterers (Luke 18:9-14). Because they fasted twice a week and tithed their money, they thought that was enough to please God. However, the person that knows they require mercy from God is the one who God is pleased with (Luke 18:13-14).

Be careful of the unforgivable sin

Among the many miracles that Jesus performed while He was on the earth, He healed a demon-possessed man who was blind and unable to speak (Matthew 12:22). While the majority of the people were astonished and wondered if Jesus was the Messiah, God's chosen one, the Pharisees crossed the line and assigned the work of the Holy Spirit to Satan (Matthew 12:24). Sins against the Holy Spirit are beyond forgiveness. Indeed, Jesus refers to these Jews as the synagogue of Satan (Revelation 2:9). At the centre of the sin is enormous pride, prejudice and stubbornness to believe that the miracles Jesus performed came from God.

My worry and concern are that similar sins may occur in our churches. I have heard more often than I want to recount people coming out of church after a service only to state that the Holy Spirit was not present in the service today. Be very careful here because I have heard others coming out of the same service saying that the Holy Spirit really spoke to them, and on occasion, the Holy Spirit touched their hearts so much that it changed their lives. Even though God did not speak to you today, He may have spoken to others. We will have to give account for every idle word we have spoken (Matthew 12:36-37). This alone should help us remain humble and know that we need the mercy of God to pass through to eternal life.

After the Pharisees had accused Jesus of being demon-possessed, Jesus began to speak in parables to the Jews because the secrets of the Kingdom of God had been taken away from them (Matthew 13:10-13).

Parables of the Kingdom of God

Parable of the Weeds (Matthew 13:36-43): In this section and the next chapter, we will look at some of the parables of Jesus and examine what they mean for us today. What is the Kingdom of Heaven like? The Kingdom of Heaven, as it is seen in the world, has two populations: the wheat, who are those who follow Jesus and the weeds, those who remain in darkness (Matthew 13: 24-30). In this parable, good, as represented by the wheat and evil, as represented by the weeds, have to grow to maturity side by side. Therefore, things are going to get worse in the world until the weeds are pulled out and separated from the good. The weeds are the children of Satan, and their destiny is to be burnt in the fire (Matthew 13:37-40). The weeds have to be burnt in the fire of hell before the righteous are able to shine as the sun. The righteous and wickedness do not have anything in common, but both populations currently occupy the world (2 Corinthians 6:14). Enoch prophesied against the wicked that God would come to convict the ungodly against all their ungodly deeds. (Jude 14-16). Jude prophesied that in the last days of this age that ungodliness would get worse (Jude 17-19).

Hidden treasure (Matthew 13:44-45): In this parable, Jesus shows us the things of the Kingdom of God are like hidden treasure. How do we view the Kingdom of God? Are we excited that we are part of God's Kingdom and that we have found hidden treasure? Are we prepared to sell everything we have to enter the Kingdom of God? Or do we take everything that Jesus has done for us for granted? Have our hearts grown cold? (Matthew 24:12). Have we become too over-familiar with God and with what Jesus has done for us to bring us into the Kingdom of God? Do we know that God has blessed us with every spiritual blessing in Christ, and are we taking hold of these blessings and making them our own? (Ephesians 1:3). There are terrible times ahead of us as we are surrounded by people who love themselves, are greedy for money, unholy, ungrateful for what they have, lacking in self-control, only love the pleasures of life, have a form of godliness but deny the power of the cross and resurrection (2 Timothy 3:1-5). We are clearly living in these times, and therefore it is more important than ever to take hold of the treasure of the Kingdom of God.

Parable of the net (Matthew 13:47-52): We should be aware that in this parable, Jesus restates that at the end of this age, the angels will come to separate the righteous from the wicked. They will throw the wicked into the furnace of hell, where there will be much pain and suffering. We need to ensure that we are considered to be with the righteous and that we have truly entered the Kingdom of God because a terrible future awaits those who have rejected God. Store up our treasure in heaven so that we have an inheritance in the Kingdom of God (Matthew 6:19-21).

Parable of the wedding banquet (Matthew 22:1-14): Jesus has invited us to the wedding banquet that is within the Kingdom of God. Are we among those who are coming to the banquet? Are we among those that care more about our earthly jobs and everyday living? To enter the banquet of God, we must ensure that we are clothed with the righteousness of God that is only found through the Lord Jesus Christ. All those who haven't received Jesus as their Lord and Saviour will be thrown outside into the darkness of eternal suffering (Matthew 22:12-13). We have been warned that many are invited to God's banquet, but few are chosen to be worthy of the Kingdom of God (Matthew 22:14).

Parable of the mustard seed and yeast (Luke 13:18-20):
Jesus expects the Kingdom of God to grow. A mustard seed is a very small seed, and that is what is sown in the hearts of those who believe in Jesus as their Lord and Saviour. However, the mustard seed, once planted in our hearts, must grow, and when it grows, it becomes a huge tree that brings blessings to others. How many talents has God given to us (Matthew 25:14-30)? If God has given us many or few talents, have we put our talents to good use, and are we using our talents to grow the Kingdom of God? To those who use their talents for God, more will be given to them, but to those who waste their talents and bury them in the ground, even the little they have will be taken from them (Matthew 25:29-30).

The purpose of the selected parables I have shown here is that our focus in this life should be on Jesus and not on worldly pursuits. In such a demanding and intense world, it is very easy to be distracted from our purpose in being here, to follow the world's lead and go after the perishable things that ultimately will come to nothing. The central message that we keep returning to is that, in these last days of this age, we should focus our minds and efforts on heavenly things above and store up our treasure in heaven.

Prayer

Dear Lord Jesus, we thank You that You have shown us how to deal with conflict and misfortune in our lives. We also thank You that You have not left us alone but have provided Your Holy Spirit to lead us in all truth through this difficult world. We praise and worship You for showing us through your parables what the Kingdom of God is like and how precious being a part of God's Kingdom is. Help us never to lose sight of the promised land of eternal life through Your saving grace. Help us not to look at the waves of the water around us or the storms of life but to keep our eyes totally and completely on You so that we may rise above the challenges and storms of this life in the world. In Jesus's name, we pray, Amen.

The lost and found department

Jesus told many parables to illustrate different truths. In Luke 15:8-10, Jesus told the parable of the lost coin to illustrate what it is like in heaven when one person turns from darkness into the light of becoming a believer in Jesus Christ as their Lord and Saviour. The question is, what do we see when we look at this very short parable of just three verses some 2000 years after Jesus first told the story? A woman with ten silver coins loses one, so she cleans her house until she finds the coin. Consequently, she rejoices and tells her friends and neighbours that she has recovered the lost coin. The illustration is that similar rejoicing occurs among God and the angels in heaven over a single sinner who crosses into the Kingdom of God. Each person saved from the coming destruction of the earth and the judgement and anger of God at the lawlessness of the world is a basis of great joy in heaven. It's often something that, in my experience, is skimmed over or given superficial attention as a stepping stone to the two longer parables on either side.

But as the filling in the sandwich is important for the taste, so is this parable for us to fully understand what Jesus is trying to communicate in these parables. Part of the problem is that, in our culture, we identify more easily with the parable of the lost sheep and the parable of the prodigal son and merciful father than we do with the parable of the lost coin. However, the more we look at the parables, the more they have to say to us. And the wonder of God's word is the more we seek, the more we find.

Parable of the lost sheep (Luke 15:1-7)

In the parable of the lost sheep, there is something we immediately warm to, which is that the shepherd does the work. It's great to have the blessing of being in God's Kingdom but not having to do anything. We identify with the human condition: we, like sheep, have all gone astray - each on our own path. There is no accountability; we can go and get lost, and Jesus will come and find us. If that's what we believe, then we miss the point.

We can easily see Jesus as the shepherd. John tells us, 'I know my sheep, and my sheep know me.' We can identify with the vulnerability; the world is a difficult place to live, and it is becoming more dangerous. However, notice that the shepherd leaves 99 sheep in the open field to go and look for the lost sheep. The shepherd goes looking for the sheep and does not give up until he finds him. The parable tells of the incredible love of God.

I'm sure you are familiar with John 3:16. God loved the world so much that he provided his one and only Son as a replacement for our rebellion, sins and transgressions. Everyone who accepts Jesus as their Lord and Saviour shall not go to eternal damnation where there is much suffering but rather will cross over from death and condemnation to eternal life. Notice that God *loved* the world. It is in the past tense, indicating that it is a one-off single offer from

God. This is the good news of the gospel, but it is only the beginning. God follows this up by declaring to us that no eye has seen, no ear has heard, or no mind has conceived what God has prepared for those who love him, but God has revealed it to us by his Spirit (1 Corinthians 2:9-10). In the 21st century, there is a familiarity with God which means we have lost the wonder and enormity of what God, through Christ, has done for us. Words cannot convey the love God has for us and what God has planned for those who are saved.

The prayer of faith (Ephesians 3:16-19)

When we think of the church here in our locality or the wider church in the United Kingdom, Australia, Europe, Canada, United States or in our home country, whichever other that may be, how do we pray? Paul prayed, "I pray that out of His glorious riches, He may strengthen you with power through His Spirit in your inner being, so that Christ may dwell in your hearts through faith." We all need strength. And we all need to have Christ dwell in our hearts. The prayer continues, "And I pray that you, being rooted and established in love, ..." What a transformation would take place in the church and in the world if we were all rooted and established in love and may have power together with all the Saints. The prayer would be outstanding if it ended just there, but it doesn't, and this is the final line. "To grasp how wide and long and high and deep is the love of Christ, and to know this love that surpasses knowledge, sothat you may be filled with the measure of all the fullness of God."

Have we grasped how wide and long and high and deep Christ's love really is? To go back to the parable of the lost sheep, in verse 7, there is more rejoicing in heaven over one sinner who repents than in 99 who are righteous. What makes God happy? One sinner who repents - that makes God happy.

When he was dying, the great scientist Sir Michael Faraday was asked about his speculations for life after death. His reply was, "Speculations. I know nothing about speculations; I'm resting on certainties. I know that my redeemer lives, and because he lives, I live also (Job 19:25).[34]

That's where we stand. We should know about our certainties that those who believe in Christ will in no way be put aside. We have eternal life. BUT what of the lost? What hope do they possess?

One of my favourite preachers is George Whitfield. He was a contemporary of Charles Wesley, and I read somewhere a long time ago that when Whitfield preached, he did so with streams of tears running from his eyes. The reason was that when he was a young man, God took him to hell and showed him all that dwelt there. Whitfield never forgot the experience and knew that if he didn't get his message across, that was the fate of all who heard him. Woody Allen, the well-known filmmaker, said, *"It's not that I'm afraid to die; I just don't want to be there when it happens."*[35] *The last words that Queen Elizabeth I is reported to have uttered were, "All my possessions for a moment in time."*[36]

As Jesus challenged us, 'What shall it profit any man to gain the world but lose his soul?' I believe the church has lost its sense of purpose over recent decades. That sense of purpose today may

34 1500 Illustrations for Biblical Preaching, page 121. Edited by Michael P Green. Baker Books, Grand Rapids Michigan, USA, 2001.

35 The Little Oxford Dictionary of Quotations, page 91. Second Edition edited by Susan Ratcliffe with Helen Rappaport, 2001.

36 The Little Oxford Dictionary of Quotations, page 198. Second Edition edited by Susan Ratcliffe with Helen Rappaport, 2001.

be the last chance many people have of finding Christ. God rejoices over one sinner saved because it's one less person he has to send to hell. We have lost the vision of what a terrible place hell is. We have become comfortable with our own situation and have forgotten the purpose; we are here to spread the good news of the gospel.

The Parable of the Prodigal son (Luke 15:11-32)

Again, it is easy to identify with the parable of the merciful father and the prodigal son, depending on your view. It's quite difficult to be a parent. We all hope and pray that our children turn out OK. We become anxious when we see them making the same mistakes we made, and there is a sense of relief when and if they get it reasonably right and choose the right path to Christ, have a decent job and an acceptable life partner.

So, there is a lot that we recognise in the son that turns away; it reminds us of someone we know very well. That someone is ourselves. We blow it, end up in a pigsty lifestyle and then come crawling back to God, and our merciful Father takes us back.

It shows God's patience in having to let us go when we want our way rather than His way. The parable speaks so much of the condition of modern Britain. We have lost our way; we no longer can consider ourselves a Christian country. There is less and less accountability, and we are degenerating into an ever-increasing lawless society.

Teenagers in the UK turning to crime is occurring more frequently. Knife crime and murder are becoming all too common, and the prisons cannot contain all those who need to be sent there.

It should shock us how low humans can stoop and how evil they can become when the constraints of what is right and wrong are removed. The point of the parable of the prodigal son is that no matter how far we fall away and how deep a pit we sink into, God waits to restore us. He is actively looking out for us to return to him. God can always reach us if we are willing to repent, but the choice is ours. God has a purpose for our lives, but we have a choice. We can go our own way, or we can go God's; there is no in-between and no other road to take. We have the broad, easy road that leads to destruction, or we have the very narrow road that leads to eternal life.

So, then, we come to the filling in the sandwich of the two longer parables: the parable of the lost coin (Luke 15:8-10). On the surface, the parable is easy to understand. A woman has ten coins, and she loses one. She cleans the house from top to bottom until she finds it, then throws a party for her friends and neighbours to rejoice. Likewise, there is rejoicing in the presence of the angels over one sinner saved. The word translated by modern translations as a silver coin is *drachma* in Greek, and it had a street value of approximately 14p.[37] However, if we take the rate of inflation into account and calculate average inflation at a rate of between 5% and 10%, today, we would be looking at between £1400 and £2800. This is not a huge amount of money by today's value, but significant enough to be missed if lost.

Anybody who has ever lost anything, particularly if it is important, will identify with what the woman is experiencing here. I don't know about you guys, but I'm always losing things, and it's frustrating. Yet,

---

37 The New Bible Dictionary, Money, pages 836-841. Organising editor J D Douglas, InterVarsity Press, 1962, reprinted 1974.

if it's something valuable, then it causes a lot of anxiety until I can find what I did with it.

Firstly, we have a woman who lives on her own; there is no man to clutter things up or to get in the way and make matters worse. The point is that God sees us as individuals with real needs. It's so human to misplace things and lose them. The number ten in the Bible is the number of completeness, and if we lose 10%, then we are not complete. The number one in the Bible is considered by some to be the amount of unity.[38] So, in a subtle way, the parable is pointing to the human condition. In the fall from grace, mankind lost something that makes us incomplete we lost our true position and our true identity. We are no longer the people God created us to be.

Repentance in the new world order

The most important thing we lost was our relationship with God. Those that love the Lord and obey his commands are told that Christ comes and lives inside of us. That is a fundamental belief of Christianity; we are reconciled with God, and part of that process entails God living in us.

But central to these parables is the concept of repentance. As discussed earlier in this book, it's a concept that is not popular in our culture or across the Western world today. However, it is essential that we grasp the importance of keeping clean sheets with God. So, it is vital that we grasp the meaning of repentance. According to the New Bible Dictionary, repentance means *"to turn or return and is applied in turning from sin to God."* In the Old Testament, this results

---

38 A Grün. Jesus: The Image of Humanity: Luke's Account, pages 55-58. Continuum, New York, 2003.

in a change not only on the human side but on God's side, too; we move out of His judgement into His grace.[39]

In the New Testament, repentance usually refers to a change of mind. We no longer chase after the things of the world, but we renew our minds to follow the ways of God. Our goals become the goals of furthering the Kingdom of God. Repentance is an essential requirement for becoming a Christian. It's not an option. Not so very long ago, we used to have fire and brimstone preachers who used to frighten people into the Kingdom of God, and as a preacher, I have an interest in how it used to be done.

I like to read books by people like J.C Ryle, who was appointed the first bishop of Liverpool in 1880 and was around until 1900. Andrew Murray wrote from the 1840s to around 1910, and Charles Spurgeon, (1834 to 1892). Their books have had such an impact they are still around today. Go back even further and read the works of Thomas Watson from the 17th century, or come forward to read A.W Tozer, who died in 1963. All these men had a great impact on their generation, and central to their messages is the need to repent. 2 Chronicles 7:14 says, *"If my people who are called by my name, will humble themselves and pray and seek my face and turn from their wicked ways, then will I hear from heaven and will forgive their sin and will heal their land."* Yet, revival tarries and has not come because we have failed to grasp the importance of repentance to God. The emphasis is on us. We need to repent from our sins, and I would suggest that this verse indicates that repentance is more than a once and for all decision.

---

39 The New Bible Dictionary, Money, pages 1083-1084. Organising editor J D Douglas, InterVarsity Press, 1962, reprinted 1974.

"If my people who are called by my name will humble themselves." *God is not talking to the world here; he is talking to us. We need to turn, humble ourselves, repent, pray and seek His face. The message is clear. Do we have difficulties hearing what God is trying to say to us? Then listen up. Romans 12:2 says, "Do not conform any longer to the pattern of this world, but be transformed by the renewing of your mind. Then you will be able to test what God's will is - His good, pleasing and perfect will."* Renew our thinking, humble ourselves and change direction. In other words, get right with God. When we do these things, then there is much rejoicing in heaven. But that's not all. Repentance changes us; it makes us whole, and it renews our relationship with God. As the parable states, when the house that is our body is cleansed, we find what is missing; the treasure that was lost is found. The light of the Holy Spirit begins to work all over again in our lives; we begin to see things again like we did when we first started out. Staying in a right relationship with God is important because we are never truly at peace unless we are right with God. If we harbour sin in our hearts, then our relationship with God is damaged.

God has promised to all who have sinned and repent that he will forgive our wickedness and remember our sins no more (Hebrews 8:12). Repentance gives us a fresh start with God; it wipes the slate clean. If we confess our sins, we have an advocate with the Father who intercedes on our behalf. God does not remember our wrongdoings. That is the good news of the gospel. All who repent will be forgiven, as God forgives our wickedness.

Evil is a word that man is trying to eliminate from the dictionary. People who murder are seldom called evil anymore; they are called victims. Scientists are trying to prove that those who commit the most atrocious crimes do so because of some flaw in their genetic makeup. In other words, it's not their fault. However, the Bible has a different perspective; those who sin are called wicked. Those who rebel against God are called evil. One Sunday school teacher was trying to teach her Sunday school class about sins of commission and sins of omission and asked if anyone knew what sins of omission are. One child replied that sins of omission are sins you'd like to do but haven't got around to them yet.[40]

The Bible speaks of time being short; a man born of a woman is of a few days and full of trouble (Job 14:1). He springs up like a flower and withers away, like a fleeting shadow he does not endure. Time is short for us to come into a right relationship with God. The world and its desires will pass away, but the man who does the will of God lives forever. That's the good news. The man who does the world of God will live forever. I have no idea of your priorities today, but we are all under pressure to succeed and conform to the world's desires and standards. Let us not conform to the world but come out and be separated. To come out and live solely according to God's standards and his direction.

The night is nearly over; the day is almost here. So let us put aside the deeds of darkness and put on the armour of light (Romans 13:12). Everyone one of us will come before the judgement seat of God. On that day, let us be in a position where God says to us,

---

40 McHenry's Stories for the Soul, page 1540. Hendrickson's Publishers, USA.

"Come up here, you good and faithful servant, and receive your reward.

To find that which is lost from our life is a great cause of celebration. To walk in a right relationship with God is pure joy. Let us press on to know the Lord.

Prayer

Dear Heavenly Father, it is so good to know how precious we are to You and that our redeemer lives. It is so good to know that You are waiting to welcome us into eternal life. Lord, there is nothing we value on this earth more than You, and the gift of eternal life is the most precious and wonderful gift there is. Help us to repent of our worldly passions and desires so that we may be rooted and established in your love. Dearest precious Lord, help us to grasp how wide, long, high, and deep is the love of Christ. Help us to receive all that You have prepared and promised us in this life. We thank you, Father, that there is more rejoicing in heaven over a single sinner saved than for 99 righteous people. Enable us to partake in the joy of seeing sinners saved, whether they be our family, neighbours, work colleagues or just acquaintances. In Jesus's name, we pray, Amen.

The way of the cross

Jesus's commandment to His followers is that if anyone wanted to be a disciple, each day, they would have to take up the cross and follow Him (Luke 9:23). The conundrum here is that if we want to be safe and hold onto our life, ultimately, we will lose it. However, if we relinquish the rights over our life and surrender to Jesus, we will gain eternal life (Luke 9:24). We tend to hold out on Jesus because we fear what surrendering everything to Jesus would actually mean for us. Stepping out into the unknown with Jesus is something that can scare us. Yet, in reality, it is the safest thing we can do because Jesus knows us better than we know ourselves. He knows how to lead, for the Lord is my shepherd, and we shall not lack or want anything. If we are tired and worn out by the trials and demands of life, we should come to Jesus for rest, take Jesus's yoke upon us and bring it into our lives. Jesus is gentle and humble and has a heart of love toward us. We will find rest for our weary souls, for Jesus's demands and burdens are light compared with the demands of the world (Matthew 11:28-30).

The journey toward the cross

As Jesus sets out for Jerusalem, he already knows that he will be betrayed by one of his disciples and that the journey will end in the crucifixion on the cross (Luke 9:44). All of us are on a journey with God; either our journey will end in eternal life or in God's judgement and eternal damnation which is hell. We need to keep our eyes on the road ahead and not worry about past decisions or what we left behind when we started our journey with God (Luke 9:62). Sitting at the Lord's feet and learning from Him is the better option rather than being taken up with the hustle and bustle of daily living in the world (Luke 10:40-42).

It is important that we are honest with ourselves before God and men, because we will be found for any hypocrisy we hide in our hearts (Luke 12: 2-5). We cannot hide anything from God, and it is perhaps amazing that we try to conceal our inner thoughts or the careless words we have spoken. God will reveal all. Chasing after wealth and more possessions is futile, and it is a large distraction on our journey with God (Luke 12:15-21). Let us be rich toward God and seek after the things that are important to God. We are called to interpret what is happening in God's world (Luke 12:56). As Jesus continued his journey toward Jerusalem and the cross (Luke 13:22), He warned us again about making sure that we were on the correct road with Jesus. Enter through the narrow door because many will not be able to enter (Luke 13:24-28).

On the journey to Jerusalem, Jesus not only found time to teach but also to continue to do the work of God (Luke 17:11-19). It is important that we retain a grateful heart for all that God is doing in our lives (Luke 17:17-19). The gospel message is to be ready for the unexpected. When Jesus returns, he will come quickly and without warning. Those who have remained in him and continued with perseverance and a prepared heart will be taken to be with him in paradise (Luke 17:33-37). Jesus warns his disciples of what lies ahead regarding the cross (Luke 18:31-34). As soon as Jesus entered Jerusalem, he wept over the city because they did not recognise Jesus as the Messiah (Luke 19:41-44). The struggle of Jesus takes place on the Mount of Olives, asking his Father to relinquish him from the coming ordeal of the cross (Luke 22:39-45). The crucifixion is followed by the empty tomb at the resurrection of our Lord and Saviour.

Message of the cross

The message of the cross is the power of God for those who are believers and have entered into the Kingdom of God, but it is absurdly crazy to those who are destined for hell (1 Corinthians 1:18). Nevertheless, the cross remains at the centre of the gospel message. Without the cross, there is no resurrection and no hope of eternal life. Without the cross, there is no forgiveness of sins and no reconciliation with Almighty God.

We are called to run the course of the race that God has set us upon, and to discard everything that gets in the way of our journey with God (Hebrews 12:1). This can only be accomplished by fixing our eyes upon our Lord and Saviour and to acknowledge the shame that Jesus endured upon the cross (Hebrews 12:2). The things of the world are crucified and defeated through the cross of Christ; this is the Christian way of life (Galatians 6:14). The Apostle Paul tearfully acknowledged that many people live their lives as enemies of the cross of Christ (Philippians 3:18). Those who are called to eternal life live a life that is crucified to worldly gain (Galatians 2:20, 5:24). They have crucified the sinful nature and natural desires of this world

(Galatians 5:24). We have peace through the blood of Jesus that was sacrificed on the cross (Colossians 1:19-20). Indeed, Christ is the atoning sacrifice for our sins and the sins of the whole world (1 John 2:2). The cross is for those whose lives have fallen apart and can relate to Jesus's cry on the cross, *"My God, my God, why have you forsaken me?"* (Matthew 27:46)[41] This is the anguish of those who have lost all hope in life and know only total despair. Jesus knew sorrow, and the grief of life and being separated from God was unique for Jesus as He was the only person who truly knew the Father. Anyone who has seen Jesus has seen the Father. What do we remember and see when we think of Good Friday? Do we think of the fear of political and religious leaders who struggle with a deteriorating world, who struggle with the discontent of the people? Politicians who have no solutions to the rising costs of living, who are failing to help people on the breadline of life, and people who are failing to make ends meet. Do we remember that the leaders in Jesus's day sent the Lord to the cross because they feared an uprising of the people?[42] Good Friday is not the end because it is quickly followed by Easter Sunday and a time that those who despair in this life may see the resurrection and the future hope of better things that Jesus truly offers.[43]

According to Matera, Israel's rejection of the Messiah and their cry that they have no King other than Caesar (John 19:15-16) resulted in the transference of God's Kingdom to the church.[44] This occurs with the tearing of the curtain in the holy of holies in the Temple of

41 Brian Haymes. Looking at the Cross, pages 104-105. International Bible Reading Association, Surrey, UK. 1988.
42 Haymes, IBID, pages 105-106.
43 Haymes, IBID, page 108.
44 Frank J. Matera. Chapter 6, Part III, page 136. God's new nation the church.. In Passion Narratives and Gospel Theologies:. Wipf and Stock Publishers, Oregon, USA. 2001.

Jerusalem. The death of Jesus also coincides with the first fruits of the resurrection of mankind; the repentant thief is resurrected to a life in paradise with Jesus (Luke 23:42-43). The tombs of many Saints were opened, and they were able to go through Jerusalem, appearing to many people (Matthew 27:50-53). It is clear that a new era had arrived; the old had gone, the new had come. Subsequently, Jesus, after His resurrection, commissions us to go to make disciples of all nations, baptising them in the name of the Father, the Son and the Holy Spirit (Matthew 28:19-20). Therefore, the Gentiles were accepted into God's Kingdom (Acts 10:1-48).

As Derek Prince has summarised, the truth of the cross was a divine exchange which unlocked the treasures of the Kingdom of God for those who believed.[45] Jesus was punished that we might be forgiven; He was wounded that we might be healed; He was made sin for our sinfulness that we might exchange our sin for His righteousness; He died our death that we may share His life; Jesus was cursed for us that we may live in blessing; He endured poverty that we may access His riches; he bore our shame that we may enjoy His glory; He was rejected that we may be accepted; our old life died that we may be resurrected into the new life with the Holy Spirit.[46]

We have been delivered from the evil one and this present evil world, from the Old Testament law, from our selfish ways, from our fleshly desires and from the temptations of the world.[47]

---

45   Derek Prince. Atonement, page 37. Derek Prince Ministries, Hertfordshire, UK. 2000.
46   Prince, IBID, page 37.
47   Prince, IBID, page 38.

Prayer

Dearest Lord Jesus, thank you for the cross and the suffering that You went through so that I may be saved and inherit eternal life. Thank you that I have been saved by the grace of God, not through my own efforts or works but through the saving grace that is the cross. Dear Lord, never let us forget what You have done for each one of us so that we may enter into God's family. Thank you, Lord, that You were punished that we might be forgiven; that You were wounded that we might be healed; that You were made sin for our sinfulness that we might exchange our sin for your righteousness; that You suffered and died a terrible death on our behalf that we may share your eternal life; that You were cursed for us that we may live in blessing; that You gave up heavenly riches and endured poverty that we may have access to Your riches and every spiritual blessing in the heavenly realms; that You bore our shame that we may enjoy and partake in Your glory; that You were rejected that we may be accepted. Thank you that through the cross, our old life died so that we may be resurrected into the new life with the Holy Spirit. In Jesus's name, we pray, Amen.

The righteous shall live by faith

What is faith?

Faith is believing in something that cannot be seen or hasn't even come into existence yet because it is in the future (Hebrews 11:1). We believe that, through Jesus Christ, we are saved from our sins. At some point in the future, we will go to heaven to be with the Lord; that is the centre or pillar of our faith. When it comes to faith, we all have much more faith than we sometimes believe we have. When we begin to think about what we believe in, most of us believe that there is a God. Even though we have not seen Him, we have faith that He is there. We believe that there is a heaven and a place called hell. We believe that all who accept Jesus Christ as Lord and Saviour will be saved from God's eternal judgement (Romans 10:13). We also believe that Jesus will come back again soon and that all who believe in him and call upon His name as our Lord and Saviour will reign with Him in paradise. All of these things are in the future, and we rely on our faith to believe that, one day, they will come true. We believe that the Bible is the inspired word of God and that God communicates with His people through the living word of God (2 Timothy 3:16).

We use our faith every day whenever we pray or spend time with God; we have faith that He is there and listens to our prayers. At important times in our lives, we exercise faith, for example, when trying to find His will on whether or not we should move jobs, who we should marry, what area to live in or which college we should go to. There are an infinite number of ways that we exercise faith, and we almost always use faith when we seek God at difficult times in our lives. Faith becomes even more important during the difficult times when God doesn't seem to answer, or the answer is no. Our faith can be tested sometimes to breaking point, especially when praying for someone who is ill or for a loved one who is in trouble. At these times, we need to persevere and trust that God's ways are the best way and, ultimately, He will bring us through the heartbreak times.

Faith is continuing with God when all the circumstances tell us otherwise. Faith is continuing to trust God when we feel betrayed, let down and when all we want to say is, *"Why, God?"* 'If only you'd been here when I needed you the most, things would have turned out differently' is a statement that has been said many times by others (John 11:17-32). Almost always, the answer to your why question is that what you have experienced is to bring glory to God and to show the world that God is there (John 11:4-6). The most important point here is that whenever we go through the darkest of times - when our faith is tested the most, even to the point that we question our beliefs - it is because God loves you very much, and He has a higher purpose for your life.

Faith is at its strongest when believing occurs through adversity. Sometimes God answers quickly, and our faith is rewarded almost before we have finished asking. At other times, the answer seems to take forever, and there is a long wait between the prayer and the answer. Faith is bringing into existence things that are at this moment in the future and unseen. Most importantly, faith is the currency of heaven. It is more valuable in God's sight than the most precious metals that we have on the earth, such as gold and silver, and by today's standards, more precious than platinum (1 Peter 1:7). The Lord will test our faith to see if it is genuine and if it is based upon Him (James 1:3). Like gold has to be refined in a furnace to get rid of impurities, our faith also needs to be refined to ensure that it is pure. It is for these reasons that we need to learn to understand and value our faith because of its very precious nature. It also means that we need to stop thinking like the world thinks and renew our thinking to understand what is important to God.

How does faith come into being?

Faith comes into being by hearing the word of God (Romans 10:17). There are many different ways that we can hear the word of God. We can hear the word of God when we read the Bible; sometimes, a verse just jumps out of the page and hits us in the face. We feel in our hearts that God has just spoken to us; there is a real sense of excitement. Faith will be strengthened at such times. Sometimes, when we are doing other things, the word of God flutters into our minds like a butterfly settling on a flower. God reminds us of a truth that we may have forgotten, or something begins to sink into our hearts when we are reading the Bible that has an impact on our faith without us even realising that it has happened.

We may be listening to others speaking the word, either through a sermon or in a group Bible study, when the Holy Spirit brings something to our attention, and we know that it is a word from God. The Lord can speak through a hymn or a chorus when we are listening to Christian music. The word of God can even inspire through nature when we are out in the countryside. There are many different ways that we can hear from the Lord. The exciting things are that God speaks to us today and uses the way that is best for us, as we all have different personalities and characteristics that make us unique.

Consider the different ways that God spoke to people in the Bible, and the variety is amazing. God spoke to Adam and Eve in a garden (Genesis 3:8-9), Enoch while walking with him (Genesis 5:22-24), to Abraham in a vision (Genesis 15:1), to Jacob in a dream (Genesis 28:12), to Elijah through a small voice (1 Kings 19:12-13), and to Nehemiah through the testimony of others and the word of God (Nehemiah 1:3-15). There are many ways that God speaks to us, His servants, and the reality is that He does speak to us.

What type of faith do we have?

Even the smallest amount of faith can achieve incredible things and have a massive impact on our own lives, on our families, our friends, the people around us, our churches and our nations (Matthew 17:20). The Bible tells us that we can move mountains with even the smallest grain of faith. Trust me when I say that mountains can appear in many shapes and forms and, to the human eye, they can appear as enormous as physical giants. We can approach a mountain from the bottom and be daunted by the enormity of the object. A fleck of faith can move the mountain into the sea, and it will be removed from our path and from view forever, gone, destroyed. We come to a point where we have to believe what the Lord has said. That is faith: Jesus said it, I believe it, and therefore it shall come into being and happen.

The question is, why are we not seeing and experiencing mountain-moving activity in our homes, communities, churches and nations? Could it be that we are not taking hold of what we already have possession of, and therefore we are allowing Satan to gain ground he has no right to? Are we too concerned with the world to be effective ambassadors for God on the earth? It is likely that we do not pray for the mountains to move, or we are unaware that we need to move the mountain and any other obstacle that is placed in the way of God's purposes for our lives and the lives of those we can influence.

God isn't content for us to have only a speck of faith. His desire is that our faith is a seed that grows into a great big tree of faith (Matthew 17:20). Indeed, the Bible teaches that if our faith grows, then nothing will be impossible for us to achieve. Yet, we appear far from that position and even hamstrung into inactivity. So, the question remains: what kind of faith do we want to have? Even a mustard seed of faith can achieve great things, but imagine what could be achieved if we took hold of the promise and allowed our faith to grow into a mustard tree.

What are the obstacles to achieving mustard tree faith? Firstly, doubt or unbelief that we can achieve what the word of God has promised we can achieve and, linked to this, a desire to want the kind of faith that can change our generation. We are looking for the type of faith that is centred on God's desires so that the impurities of this life are put aside and become irrelevant. We are no longer focusing on the daily problems and struggles of life but are truly focused on the Lord. We begin to pray that God shows us His desires and what is important to Him for our families, churches, communities and nation. To grow in faith takes time in prayer, seeking His will, and then all things will be added to us (Matthew 7:7-8).

Growing in faith

To grow in faith, we first have to seek God's Kingdom and align our desires with His desires (Matthew 7:7-8). The Lord desires that we commit our way to Him and trust Him (Psalm 37:5-8). Faith grows when we stop believing in the circumstances and move our focus into trusting Him, no matter what and no matter how long it takes to achieve whatever we are waiting for. Keep on trusting and trusting and trusting. God also desires righteousness, which is that we are perfect, and that is achieved through our position in Christ (Romans 3:21-26). The Lord also wants us to wait for Him and not rush ahead of His timing. While we are waiting for the answer to come, whatever that may be, God wants us to rest. It is all too easy in the instant world we live in to become anxious and worried when we don't get instant answers to our prayers. We start to get worried, and the temptation is that we reach out and take for ourselves what we believe is the right thing without waiting for God to answer. What is good in our eyes is often not God's best for our lives. We should never settle for second best because, in the long term, it will damage our faith and lead to discontentment and regrets. Waiting for God's timing is always the very best solution, even if we don't understand why God is taking so long. Don't fret, don't worry, the answer is coming.

Being in harmony with God is the surest and only way to grow in faith and reach a place where we are mustard trees, not simply the seeds. During times of waiting, exercise faith by asking the Lord for verses that can help faith grow and strengthen during the quiet period.

Listening to the Lord

Waiting on the Lord is almost a lost virtue and gift among modern Christians who are seeking instant results in a fast-moving world. We can travel vast distances very quickly; letters that used to take weeks to deliver now arrive as emails in seconds. Mobile phones mean that we are never more than a phone call away from the next assignment or challenge. The world is moving ever quicker, and flights that once took 24 hours may be shortened to less than two hours in the future.[48] We need to learn to slow down as Christians and wait upon the Lord's timing. Don't rush ahead. The answer to whatever we have believed the Lord for will come in God's time; it won't be late.

Listening is fast becoming a lost skill. Even from the earliest age as toddlers and children, we humans find it difficult to listen. How much more difficult when the voice of the Holy Spirit comes to us

---

48 Mail Online: London to Sydney in 90 minutes: hypersonic space liner that travels at 24 times the speed of sound to be built by 2050. https://www.dailymail.co.uk/sciencetech/article-2268335/

as a whisper (1 Kings 19:12). Why come as a whisper? Why not as a thundercloud or a loud voice that would make us sit up and take notice? Probably because God wants to make sure we have His full attention and we are free from distractions. Hearing from God is so important that it demands our full attention. If there is too much background noise, we are going to miss the message.

How can we hear the whisper when there is so much noise around us? It is very difficult to find somewhere in this world that is totally quiet where we can focus and give our full attention to listening for what the Lord might want to say to us. We wouldn't want to miss something that is so important to us and the plan that God has for our life or even the answer to our prayers, which are often intertwined with our faith. Finding a quiet place we can call our own where we can meet with the Lord is so important.

Strengthening faith through listening

The most frequent way that the Lord speaks to us is through His word. It is wise to keep a record of what He is saying because when the storms come, it will determine whether we have built on sand or on rock (Matthew 7:24-27). To be able to stand on the rock of the word of God when the storms arrive means we won't get washed away. It is important to take time to listen to the voice of the Lord. The Lord has promised that regardless of our circumstances, no one can snatch us away from the Lord (John 10:27-28). We can have faith that the Lord will bring us through the dark times and our failings into victory. In all things, we can have a reassurance that God is in control of our circumstances. We can have faith that nothing is wasted in God's plan for our lives, and all we experience will enable us to grow in faith and belief. We are assured that we can depend on Almighty God to bring us safely through the waters of adversity and the fire of purification (Isaiah 43:2).

To grow in faith, we have to hear what God is saying through His word (Romans 10:17). What is God saying to us today, and are we able to hear Him? In the hectic world we live in, many have forgotten how to listen. Or maybe we listen but don't take the time to hear properly. Listening to the word of God strengthens our faith and helps it grow. It enables us to become stronger and more mature in our faith; it increases our understanding of who God is and what He has done for us. The word of God is a treasure and enables us to find the knowledge of God and also to fear the Lord (Proverbs 2:1-5). In order to listen to the word of God, there has to be a quietness that enables us to concentrate on what we are hearing from the word of God. We need to slow down and block out the world for a while so that we can listen and hear and take to heart the treasure we are receiving.

Making Faith visible

It is obvious that our faith and belief need to become more visible in the world today. We are called to be shining lights to show the lost world the way to follow (Mark 4:21). Be generous with our faith and share it with an often-despairing world. What makes us different from the world around us? What makes us stand out in the crowd? We are not all necessarily called to be evangelists and to stand in our offices on soapboxes proclaiming the way of the Lord in the way that a modern-day John the Baptist might go about things. However, if we trust the Lord and ask for opportunities to witness for him, invariably, the Lord will send someone to us who needs our help. Maybe it will be a kind word or an offer to pray for someone. It could be being sensitive to the people around us and enquiring if there is anything up when someone we come into contact with does not appear to be themselves. We shouldn't be disheartened if, at first, a person doesn't open up to us. We have sown a seed that, at some point in the future, will grow into a shoot and then into a plant that one day will bear fruit. In God, nothing is wasted, nothing goes unnoticed, nothing is ultimately in vain.

It may be many years before the seed we sow today begins to bear fruit. We are called to live our lives in the knowledge that the Lord's eyes are upon us at all times. It is amazing what the Lord can do with even the tiniest seeds of faith. God will never rush a process, and just because we cannot see anything happening doesn't mean that things aren't growing.

Consider Abraham's life and God's promise to make him the father of many nations (Genesis 17:1-7). Abraham did not live to see the fulfilment of the promise. Abraham simply believed that God would do what he had promised to do. That is the essence of our faith today; we believe that God will do what He has promised to do.

Prayer

Dear Heavenly Father, we thank You for the faith and belief You have given us in this life. We thank You that we can be pleasing to You through our faith and belief in your son, our Saviour, Jesus Christ. Thank You, Father, that if we lack faith and belief, then we can come to You and confess our lack of faith and ask You to help us in our unbelief. Thank You, Father, that the more we know you, the more we grow in faith and belief in Your glorious riches that You have promised everyone who believes. Thank you, Father, that You are there beside us in all our struggles and in our triumphs when we express the faith and belief we have in You. In Jesus's name, we pray, Amen.

The Holy Spirit as the mark of our salvation

The sign that the new era has come into the world is the anointing of the Spirit of God (Luke 3:16). Jesus provides the Holy Spirit to His followers, the Spirit of truth that will lead us into all truth (John 15:26 and 16:13). We are to preach that people need to repent and then their sins will be forgiven. However, we should not begin to preach the good news until we have received the Holy Spirit (Luke 24:49). It is clear that Jesus had to return to his Father in heaven in order to send the Holy Spirit because a human body restricted Jesus as to where he could be at any one time. The Holy Spirit can be everywhere He wishes to be and doesn't have the restrictions of being limited to a single the human body. The provision of the Holy Spirit is a sign that we are the people of God. There is a division of humanity, and the dividing line is the Holy Spirit (Ephesians 1:13).

The day of the Lord

God promised to pour out His Spirit on all believers. The young men and women, sons and daughters, would prophesy and see visions of God, and older people would dream of God, just as Joseph would see dreams and interpret them (Joel 2:28-32). God promises to show signs and wonders both in heaven and on earth. God promises that everyone who calls on the name of the Lord will be saved (Joel 2:32). This prophecy was fulfilled on the day of Pentecost, as described in Acts 2. Tongues of fire descended upon the disciples. They were filled with the Holy Spirit, and they began to speak in other languages (tongues) (Acts 2:1-4). Peter addressed the crowd and explained that the day of the Lord had arrived, as prophesied in Joel (Acts 2:15-21). Peter called the crowd to repentance and to be baptised, and 3000 people were added to the church that day (Acts 2:38-41). The signs and wonders that God promised in Joel can be seen through the healing of a crippled beggar by the Temple in Acts 3:6-8. The beggar went away praising God, and I wonder how many of us respond with such joy when God answers our prayers today. Many miraculous signs are performed in the name of Jesus (Acts 5:12-16).

It is important to remember that the baptism of the Holy Spirit is only the beginning of our relationship with Almighty God.[49] The gift of the Holy Spirit is the first fruit of the coming age in which we now live (Romans 8:3). Also, not all of Joel's prophecy has come to pass: the sun has not yet turned to darkness, nor has the moon turned to blood (Joel 2:32, Acts 2:20). This indicates that the Holy Spirit is with us until the end of this age.

From the day of Pentecost to our present day, we see, throughout history, the work of the Holy Spirit continuing the work of the Kingdom of God through believers in Christ. We see the indwelling of the Holy Spirit in the gentiles (Acts 10:44). The wisdom of the Holy Spirit upon Stephen at his martyrdom (Acts 6:10). We are

---

49 Stanley M. Horton. What the Bible Says about the Holy Spirit, page 138. Gospel Publishing House, Missouri, USA. 1995.

promised that when we are in trouble, then the Holy Spirit will come to our aid and provide the words that we require to respond to any accusations made against us (Mark 13:11). There are no weapons that can harm us, and every tongue that accuses us will be defeated (Isaiah 54:17). Everything we achieve is achieved not by might, nor by power, but by the Spirit of God (Zechariah 4:6).

Breaking down barriers

We have been saved by the grace of God. We cannot boast about our achievements because everything meaningful we have achieved has been achieved through Christ (Ephesians 2:8-10). God does not distinguish between any person. All are equal in God's Kingdom, whether we are rich or poor, male or female, Black or white, a slave or free. Regardless of our religious background or our upbringing, all are equal before God (Galatians 3:28).

The question remains, have we all received the gift of the Holy Spirit? Are we in need of being filled or indwelled by the Holy Spirit? We only have to pray and believe to receive any gift of God (James 1:5). The exciting thing is that we are on a journey through this life with the Lord, and He will not withhold anything from us that we need to fulfil our destiny. There are dark days ahead as we move toward the end of this age, but take heart. Jesus has overcome the world, and we need not fret or worry about the future, for Jesus will never leave us nor forsake us even until the end of the age (Deuteronomy 31:6-8, 1 Chronicles 28:20, Matthew 28:20, Hebrews 13:5-6).

Led by the Spirit

One of the most predominant affirmations of the working of the Holy Spirit in the lives of the church and believers is the way that we are led by the Holy Spirit.[50] We can see that Philip was led by the Holy Spirit to go south (Acts 8:26). On the road, Philip met with a eunuch. He was able to explain the gospel message to him and baptised the eunuch into the faith (Acts 8:38-39). The Holy Spirit then led Philip away and onto the road to Caesarea, where he was able to preach the gospel in many towns along the route (Acts 8:40). Barnabas and Paul are set aside to carry out the work of God by the leading of the Holy Spirit (Acts 13:1-4). Paul and Barnabas were led to many towns and cities to preach the gospel to the lost by the leading of the Holy Spirit. Paul was later led by the Holy Spirit to recognise that the leaders of the church at Ephesus were also anointed with the Holy Spirit to lead the local flock of believers forward in Christ (Acts 20:28-32).[51] Indeed, Paul was led away from areas on occasion to new challenges in Macedonia (Acts 16:6-10). The book of Acts is able to show us that the Holy Spirit wants to be involved and bound to us in every aspect of our lives, including the decisions that we have to make each day.[52]

The work of the Holy Spirit today

The Holy Spirit continues to work through individuals and churches to spread the good news of the gospel (Acts 19:10). The Holy Spirit inspires us today as much as He did at the time of the apostles.

---

50   Horton, IBID, pages 162-163.

51   Horton, IBID, page 163.

52   Horton, IBID, page 166.

The word is near to us, and the Spirit of God enables us to better understand and to know what the Lord wants to tell us (Romans 10:8). The Spirit works His seven-fold ministry today of resting upon us, providing wisdom, understanding, counsel, power, and the fear of the Lord (Isaiah 11:2). If we confess with our mouths and believe in our hearts that Jesus is Lord, we are guaranteed to be saved (Romans 10:9).

How can unbelievers be saved from the coming anger of God? They can only be saved by hearing the Spirit-inspired word of God (Romans 10:14).

When we face opposition or are in difficult situations and don't know the way forward, then we can pray in the Spirit, who will aid us in our time of need (Romans 8:26). The Spirit will search our hearts and intercede for believers in alignment with God's will (Romans 8:27). Our faith will increase in line with our understanding what God is saying to us through the word of God (Romans 10:17). In order to be delivered from the desires, we need to live in the Spirit. We must separate ourselves from the impulses and cravings of the flesh which oppose the Spirit of God (Galatians 5:16).

We are the salt of the earth, and in so many ways, the Church in the Western world has lost its saltiness and is only fit to be trampled underfoot (Matthew 5:13). We no longer hear the Church speaking out against Governmental decisions that satisfy the rich but cause disadvantage to the poor and the weak among us. God will bring judgement on the Nations who do not look after the poor among them (Proverbs 14:31, Proverbs 17:5, Amos 5:12, Zechariah 7:12). So often, the Church hides its light under a bowl and out of sight whenever the Government proposes laws that are against the will of God, and indeed, laws that are an abomination to God (Matthew 5:14-16). Our light needs to shine before men and women, especially as the darkness gathers all around the world.

The vision of the seven churches in Revelation, 2 and 3, is thought by many scholars to show the Church throughout the ages, from the resurrection of Jesus to the end of this age. However, other scholars believe that the depiction of these churches identifies the seven possible states of churches in any given state. Nevertheless, the churches have lessons for the Church in the world today. The church at Ephesus depicts the state of a lot of churches, but not all churches. In the Western world today, many churches need to rediscover their first love in order to be able to eat from the tree of life (Revelation 2:4 and 2:7). The church at Smyrna depicts those churches throughout the world that exist in countries that are opposed to Christianity. These churches should face the future without being scared, even when persecution of the Church comes to their lands, because if they overcome, they will not face the second death (Revelation 2:10-11). The church at Smyrna may also be a pillar for the rest of the world, as persecution of the Church will spread as we move toward the end of this age.

Those churches today that identify with the church at Pergamum must not think that the Church must rid itself of people who oppose the word of God or bring in heresies to appease the world. Those who overcome will be fed by God and gain a name of righteousness (Revelation 2:14-17). Those that identify with the church at Thyatira must purify themselves and not tolerate sexual immorality or occult practices, or any form of idolatry. Churches that tolerate these practices will evoke the severe judgement of the Lord (Revelation 2:20-29).

So many churches in the West believe they are alive because of the tradition of the Church or what has happened in their past history. Yet, rather than being alive, they are clearly dead, as was the church at Sardis (Revelation 3:1-6). Those who wake up in these churches and realise what is occurring will be given eternal life, but those that don't heed the word of the Lord are doomed to death.

However, for the church at Philadelphia, who has been faithful to Jesus, they are promised to be kept from the coming trials and to be protected from the synagogue of Satan (Revelation 3:7-10). The church is encouraged to hold on to what they have, which is faithfulness to Jesus. This church is promised to be a pillar in the temple of God, but God is the temple in heaven. Therefore, this promise is that the beloved from this church will dwell with God. They are also promised a new name, the name of God and the name of the new Jerusalem (Revelation 3:11-13). There are many churches in the West today that can identify with the church at Philadelphia and are attracting new converts to their churches and are both healthy and growing before the Lord.

The church at Laodicea depicts churches from many Western denominations today that are lukewarm and have a form of Christianity but deny its power. Jesus is knocking on the door of these churches today. Will the members and leaders open the door and let the Lord inside? The reward for becoming a church that is hot and on fire for the Lord is a place on the throne of God (Revelation 3:19-21).

We can be assured that the Holy Spirit is at work both in us as individuals and within the churches that allow Him to change them. Which church do we identify with today, and are we willing to allow the Spirit into our lives to move us closer to Jesus?

Prayer

Dearest Lord Jesus, thank You that You sent the Holy Spirit as a guarantee of our salvation and as an advocate to guide us through the challenges and difficulties of this life and to prepare us for the life to come. Help us, Lord, to be ever sensitive to the leading of the Holy Spirit and not to rebel or do anything to grieve the Spirit. In our daily lives, guide us never to lose our first love, to overcome all obstacles and tests that are put before us, to never let our hearts grow cold or become lukewarm, but to always be on fire for You. We thank You, Lord, that when we get stuck and do not know the way forward, we can pray in the Spirit, who will lead us into all truth. We are also thankful that whenever You feel a long way away, You are really at the door of hearts asking for permission to come in, and we invite you afresh into our hearts right now. In Jesus's name, we pray, Amen.

Jesus's prayer for his disciples

How to pray

The Bible has a lot to say about prayer, both in the Old Testament and in the New Testament. We often refer to the prayer in Matthew 5:5-15 as the Lord's Prayer, but it is really a template for believers to follow. It is clear that prayer is a private affair; don't stand on street corners or bellow out prayers in church. Rather we are to find a quiet place where we can be alone with our Heavenly Father. Prayer between God and individual believers should be rewarding, and there is no doubt that God hears the heartfelt prayers of His children. There is no need for long, convoluted prayers; prayers can be short and to the point. Many difficulties and troubles Christians face today are because we have not realised what is available to us through prayer (2 Peter 1:3).[53] The first phrases of the Lord's Prayer focus our attention upon God who is in heaven and how we should view our Heavenly Father who is holy (Matthew 5:9-10). Have we lost sight of who our God is? Has God become so familiar to us that we have lost sight of His majesty, His greatness, how awesome He is? He holds the whole universe in His hands; He is omnipotent, all-

---

53 Martyn Lloyd-Jones. The Assurance of Our Salvation: Exploring the Depth of Jesus' Prayer for His Own, pages 12-13. Crossway, Illinois, USA. 2000.

powerful, all-knowing. God is everywhere. His name is so holy that it should be revered and held above all names. Jesus is on the same level as God, who lifted Jesus to the highest place and has given him the name which is above all names (Philippians 2:9).

When we pray, we should pray in line with God's will and that God's Kingdom will be established upon the earth as it is in heaven. Only then should we pray for our needs: that we shall have sufficient food, that our sins are forgiven by our Father in heaven, and that we forgive all who have hurt us. We ask for God's mercy to lead us away from the worldly things that would tempt us to commit sins and grievances against God and others. We finally pray that God delivers us from the evil one, and we should always remember that we are not wrestling against flesh and blood but against demons in the heavenly and earthly realms. We are instructed not to worry about our lives because our lives are in the hands of God (Matthew 6:25-34). Why are so many Christians today so down and tired and living as though we are defeated?[54] If that is our template for prayer, how did Jesus approach praying for us?

The great discourse and final instructions (John 14-16)

Jesus was about to leave the disciples. He was on the way to the cross, and it was his last opportunity to share with his disciples and an opportunity to instruct all his followers throughout the ages. He began to teach and share with us in John chapter 14. He begins by instructing us not to be anxious or worried because Jesus has gone to prepare a place for each one of us in heaven (John 14:1-3). Jesus tells us that He has not forgotten us but is coming back to take us to

---

54   Martyn Lloyd-Jones, IBID, page 13.

heaven. We are reminded that everyone who has seen Jesus has seen the Father. There is no difference between God the Father and God the Son (John 14:4-10).

Jesus is not leaving us as orphans without a leader or a Saviour (John 14:18). Jesus instructs us to keep God's commandments and teaching, and He will send the Holy Spirit. Those who love Jesus will be loved by Almighty God our Father and by the Lord Jesus (John 14:21). Jesus is the source of life, and if we want to live, then we must learn to abide in Jesus and live the life that Jesus lived (John 15:1-11). Only then can we hope to live a joyous life in a world that challenges us with many troubles. It is God's will that we live a victorious life and rise above the challenges of this fallen world, and our lives should be filled with joy. We are warned that, as the world hated Jesus, the world or those of the world will hate us also. Therefore, there should be no surprise that we face trials and difficulties in this world (John 15:18-27). As Jesus overcame the world, so should we. Above all else, Jesus has left us His peace, a peace that passes all understanding (John 16:25-33).

Principles of prayer

We must remember when Jesus was praying this prayer, it was an audible prayer so that we should know what Jesus prayed for each one of us. From this prayer, we learn what our relationship is with the world and how we are to participate in the world.[55] We are here to spread the good news about salvation and who Jesus is and lead others to faith in the risen Lord.[56]

---

55 Martyn Lloyd-Jones, IBID, page 21.
56 Martyn Lloyd-Jones, IBID, page 22.

There are certain principles that define prayer. Firstly, whatever we ask for in prayer, we must believe that we have received our answer (Mark 11:24). If we lack belief, we will invariably fail to receive what we have prayed for. Secondly, pray at all times in the Holy Spirit. We need to be led by God in what we are praying for (Ephesians 6:18). Everything we ask for in prayer should be requested in Jesus's name (John 16:24). We should pray that we will escape everything that is about to happen to the world in order that we may stand before Jesus on Judgement day (Luke 21:36). Prayer opens closed doors to new possibilities and adventures in our journey with the Lord (Colossians 4:3). Pray without stopping, and in all situations, remember to give thanks to God (1 Thessalonians 5:16-18). We should give and receive encouragement from other Christians as if we are fellow prisoners with them, and especially as if we are sharing in their suffering (Hebrews 13:3). We should move away from selfishness and learn to carry each other's burdens (Galatians 6:2). In following in Jesus's footsteps, we should be aware of when Jesus prayed. Jesus went out early in the morning to pray and, on occasion, prayed all night to His Father in heaven (Luke 6:12, Mark 1:35, Luke 9:28). We pray not just to request things from God but also to ensure our contact and relationship with God, and as a foremost expression of our belief and faith in God.[57] We also should pray to discover what God is asking of us and to understand His will in our current and future circumstances. For most of us, life is a marathon, not a quick sprint, and there is no temporary or short-term escape from difficulties.

---

57   Martyn Lloyd-Jones, IBID, pages 34-35.

Jesus' prayer for every believer throughout the ages (John 17)

The prayer is divided into three sections:

1. Jesus's prayer for himself (John 17:1-5)

2. Jesus's prayer for his immediate disciples (John 17:6-19)

3. Jesus's prayer for the universal Church (John 17:20-26)

Jesus's prayer for himself

Jesus prays that He may be glorified so that the Father may be glorified (John 17:2). The whole purpose of our salvation as Christians is to glorify God and the Lord.[58] We need to live to glorify God, yet our generation has become selfish and looks for what God can give to us in material blessings and wealth. We need to get back to knowing our relationship with our Heavenly Father. God's plan for our salvation shows God's distinct character, His holiness, mercy, wisdom, love, justice and power.[59] We must never lose sight of the fact that our God reigns above all else (Psalm 97:1 and 99:1). As Jesus's time had come for the cross and resurrection, there will be an hour and a time when the time has come for God to put an end to this age. God will initiate the new age where every tear will be wiped away, and all suffering will end: a time when we will be in paradise with God.

Jesus had completed his mission and fulfilled the work that God had given him to finish. Now Jesus was returning to share in the glory of God that he had before the foundation of the world. What we long to hear from God at the end of our time and journey on the earth

---

58 Martyn Lloyd-Jones, IBID, pages 44 and 46.
59 Martyn Lloyd-Jones, IBID, page 55.

is, "Good and faithful servant, you have been faithful with the talents you were given. Come into paradise to receive so much more." (Matthew 25:21) We have lost that sense of awe and amazement at the sacrifice made for us. We have lost the vision of how great God is as captured in hymns of past generations.

Immortal, invisible, God only wise,
In light inaccessible hid from our eyes,
Most blessèd, most glorious, the Ancient of Days,
Almighty, victorious, thy great name we praise.

Unresting, unhasting, and silent as light,
Nor wanting, nor wasting, thou rulest in might;
Thy justice like mountains high soaring above
Thy clouds which are fountains of goodness and love.

To all life thou givest, to both great and small;
In all life thou livest, the true life of all;
We blossom and flourish as leaves on the tree,
And wither and perish, but nought changeth thee.

Great Father of glory, pure Father of light,
Thine angels adore thee, all veiling their sight;
All laud we would render: O help us to see
'Tis only the splendour of light hideth thee.
Walter Chalmers Smith (1824-1908)[60]

---

60   Complete Mission Praise, Marshall Pickering, London, UK. Hymn 327.

May we never lose the sense of wonder of who Almighty God is.

Jesus's prayer for His disciples

Jesus is praying for those that God has given to Him (John 17:9). Jesus is praying for those who have been elected into the family of God, the chosen ones of God who have been called according to His purposes.[61] Jesus receives glory through His disciples; therefore, we have an important role in the world (John 17:10). Jesus asks that His Father protect the disciples while they remain in the world because Jesus is going to the cross and will no longer be in the world to protect the disciples against Satan (John 17:11). As Jesus's disciples and followers, we are protected by Almighty God, and nothing can separate us from the love of God (Romans 8:28-39). As disciples of Jesus, the world hates us, and as a consequence, we must expect trouble and to be rejected by the world. Jesus was aware of the power Satan has in the world and asks our Heavenly Father to protect us from the evil one (John 17:15).

Jesus asks God to make us holy as He is holy so that we are acceptable to God and are accepted into God's family (John 17:17). All who accept Jesus and believe in Him have the right to become children of God (John 1:12-13). Therefore, we should recognise who we are in God's family. We are His children, and we are entitled to all the benefits that God has to provide. We have the right to come into the presence of Almighty God to make our supplications and prayer requests directly before Him, in Jesus's name. We are sanctified through the truth of the word of God, and it is Jesus's utmost prayer

---

61   Martyn Lloyd-Jones, IBID, page 200.

for us that we remain holy and sanctified (John 17:17-19). It is Jesus's desire that we are not tarnished or polluted by this evil world we live in but that our holiness may be complete when we meet with Jesus on His return; we will be like Him.[62]

However, Bishop J. C. Ryle pointed out in the 19th century a truth that rings true today. We live in a world of great spiritual danger. More people than ever before confess that they are Christians and believers in Christ, but have we all truly repented of our old ways, been converted and left the world behind?[63] In this respect, Bishop Ryle had ten questions to assess the spiritual position of those who believe they are true converts to Christ.[64] These questions are pertinent for every believer today:

1. Do we ever think of our spiritual position before God?

2. Do we ever do anything about our salvation?

3. Are we trying to satisfy our consciences with outward religion by doing good works?

4. Are we assured that our sins have been forgiven?

5. Have we experienced the reality of conversion into God's family?

6. Do we know anything of the practical side of holiness?

7. Do we know anything about enjoying the means of God's grace?

8. Do we ever try to do any good in the world?

9. Do we know anything about living in fellowship with Christ?

---

62 Martyn Lloyd-Jones, IBID, page 201.
63 J. C. Ryle. Walking with God, page 9. Grace Publications Trust, London, UK. 2003 edition.
64 Ryle, IBID, pages 10-14.

10. Do we know anything about being ready for the Lord's return for His disciples?

Let us not be asleep and drifting in our daily walk with Jesus. Wake up and return wholeheartedly to Jesus our Lord and Saviour.[65] It is Jesus's desire that His disciples be sanctified by God, which requires that the Holy Spirit works within us to make us aware of our sinfulness. Then it makes us aware of God's grace in wiping away our sins through the sacrifice of Jesus upon the cross and thus making us holy.[66] It is a great assurance to us that if we are true believers in Christ, then we know that the Lord is praying for us that we may be sanctified before His Father in heaven. We are to be transformed into Christ by the renewing of our minds (Romans 12:2) and to set our hearts on heavenly things (Colossians 3:2). Let us not be lovers of the world or anything in the world (1 John 2:15-17). Come out and be separate unto God. Leave our past lives behind and live the sanctified life of God.

Jesus's prayer for the universal Church

Jesus's prayer for the Church encompasses every believer throughout all the ages of the Church until he comes in the clouds with the angels for his own. It is good to know that Jesus has prayed for each one of us and is praying for us all. We should know that we are the special family of God and that our Lord cares so much about us and has such deep love for each one of us that He should pray to the Father on our behalf. It is Jesus's desire that the Church will proceed in unity, and the strength of the Church is in its united

---

65 Ryle, IBID, page 15.
66 J. C. Ryle. Aspects of Holiness, page 20. Grace Publications Trust, London, UK. 1999.

nature. However, history has shown us that it is impossible for mankind to remain in unity. From an early stage of Church history, there were schisms and divisions among the leaders of churches.[67] It is only in complete unity that the world may know that we are the people of God. It is refreshing and good to see that in recent years in England, churches are coming together in Christ to present a united gospel message.

Jesus also wants all believers to see His glory and to experience the glory that is in Christ. We can imagine something of the glory of Christ as described in the Bible. When John, the beloved disciple, met with Jesus on the Island of Patmos, he described Jesus as being dressed in a robe that reached down to his feet, with a golden sash around his chest (Revelation 1:13). His head and hair were white as snow, which shows Jesus's purity and holiness. Jesus's eyes were like a blazing fire, his feet appeared like bronze, and he had a voice like a fast-moving river (Revelation 1:14-15). Jesus's face was shining brightly like the noonday sun; it was pure and brilliant. John fell down as if dead before the brilliance of Jesus's glory. When Isaiah saw God in all His glory, he feared that he would be destroyed, so great is the glory of God (Isaiah 6:5). What convicted Isaiah of his unworthiness was all the words of his mouth. Every word that he had ever spoken could not stand in the presence of God's holiness and glory. The solution to Isaiah's dilemma was for an angel to touch his lips with burning coal to sanctify his lips, purify the words of his mouth and atone for the sin of his unclean words (Isaiah 6:6-7).

---

67   Mark A. Noll. Turning points: Decisive moments in the history of Christianity. Chapter 6. The division between east and west: The great schism. Pages 121-142. Baker Academic, Michigan, USA. 3rd edition 2012.

It is Jesus's desire that all those who know Jesus as their Lord and Saviour will be with Jesus in heaven. That is our destiny, and that is what we need to spend time meditating on. We should not look back at where we have come from, but we should look forward to that glorious day when we shall be with Jesus in all His glory. We need to be continually filled with the Holy Spirit so that we may remain in Jesus and that Jesus can remain in us (Ephesians 5:18). May the love of God fill us to overflowing each and every day. The steadfast love of the Lord never ceases, His mercies never come to an end; they are renewed each and every day, Praise God (Lamentations 3:22-23). Give, and it will be given to us in good measure, pressed down to its fullness and overflowing with God's goodness (Luke 6:38).

Prayer

Dearest Lord Jesus, thank You that You pray for me and that You know better than I do what my situation is and what my needs are. I thank You that Your steadfast love never ceases, that Your mercies never come to an end and that they are new each and every day. Thank You, Lord Jesus, that You are praying that we may be holy as You are holy, that You have gone to prepare a place for me in Your Father's house and that one day You are coming back for me that I may dwell in the house of the Lord all the days of eternity. I thank You, Lord Jesus, that when You return for me, I will be caught up in the heavens with You and that I shall be like You, fully sanctified and holy. Thank You, Lord Jesus, that You have been glorified through me, and we look forward to seeing Your brilliant light that shines like the noonday sun. In Jesus's name, we pray, Amen.

Who are we before God?

What do we do if God wants to pay us a visit?

If God declared that He was coming to your house tonight for fellowship and a chat, what would be your reaction? "Oh no, I haven't cleaned the house. I wonder if he'll notice. Or I haven't got anything to wear. I haven't got any food in. What are we going to give Him to eat? I wonder if he's had a long journey." I would want to know what He was like and particularly if He was coming as a friend or in anger. It would make a huge difference to whether or not I would be looking forward to the meeting. I wonder how we might greet God. "Hi, Lord. Great that you've dropped round. Can I get you anything? Do you need anything?"

Maybe he just wants to catch up with what's been happening in our lives. He might say, *"We haven't chatted for a while. How's life? How are you doing? Is everything OK with you? How's your family? How are the kids, the grandchildren? How's your marriage been? Tell me about your problems. Let's hang out for a while and just watch the sunset. Today is going to be one of my favourites just because I'm with you."* You might ask, *"Hey, Lord, how are things with you?" "Well, I'm still creating a few million new universes. But it's been fun. I've really enjoyed doing new things."*

We might have a lot of why questions for the Lord. *"Why did this happen, Lord?"* I think being in the presence of the Almighty, all these questions will melt away, and we will be at peace. Quietness would be enough. Time would stand still, and we would simply worship in awe and wonder.

We may enquire,"What does God think of us?"

In considering our faith and what we believe, perhaps an important question to begin with is, "What does God think of us as believers in His son Jesus the Messiah?" Our Heavenly Father, Almighty God, the creator of the universes, has categorically declared that believers in His son Jesus, who have given over their lives to His service, are His treasured possession. We are His people, and He is our God (Deuteronomy 26:18). Yet it doesn't end there because the verse states that we are to keep His commandments. In order to keep His commandments, we have to know what they are.

Before we move on to our part in salvation, we need to know that God created mankind so that He could have a family. He walked in the Garden of Eden with Adam in the cool of the evening and, by all accounts, enjoyed his time with His creation (Genesis 1:26-31).

How does God view us as His children and members of His family?

The Bible tells us that we are created in His image. Jesus could claim that whoever had seen him had seen the Father. Science tells us that in terms of the universe, man is puny and insignificant but have scientists got it right? Scientists keep pressing home the message there is only a 1% difference between an ape and man. I'm sure you've heard the claim before, but the truth is that there are over 1-2 million differences in the genetic makeup between a man and an ape; believe me, I'm very grateful for those differences. The passage before us is part of what some theological scholars call 'the covenant formula.' There have been lots of books written about the covenant formula, and scholars have done what theologians do best, which is to argue. It seems to me that some people wouldn't be happy if they didn't have something to argue about.

However, the covenant formula comes in three parts termed A, B and C.

1. PART A states simply: I will be their GOD.

2. PART B states: they will be my people.

3. PART C puts the two together to give: I will be their God, and they shall be my people.

There are a number of Bible texts that shed light on the three parts of the covenant. The central thought for us to grasp and hold onto is that God has declared, and what God declares cannot be opposed or changed. God's declaration is that we are His people; we belong to Him. We are His treasured possession; we are heavenly treasure, precious in His sight (Deuteronomy 26:18). However, the covenant comes with something we must do to maintain ourselves as God's treasured possession: keep His commands. The first requirement is to be holy as God is holy (Leviticus 11:45). Second, we are to respect our parents and observe the Sabbath (Leviticus 19:3). In these last days, we have moved away from respecting the Sabbath, and Sunday has become just another day. The Bible predicted that in the last days, there would be terrible days ahead, and part of that is that children will be disrespectful to parents (2 Timothy 3:1-5). Other things that we are instructed to obey include: not to steal, not to lie, not to deceive each other, not to profane the name of God, not to rob or defraud our neighbours, pay our bills on time, not to show any favour for the rich at the expense of the poor, not to slander people and not to hate the Christian brethren (Leviticus 19:11-17). Wouldn't the world be a better place if we Christians set about carrying out these commands and honoured other peoples' opinions above our own?

Part of being God's people requires us to consecrate ourselves and set ourselves apart for God, which requires effort on our part to ensure we don't go back to the old ways before we became Christians (Leviticus 20:7). In this respect, we must develop an attitude of repentance whenever we fall short of God's desire for our lives. God promises to walk among us and to be with us even to the end of this age (Leviticus 26:12 and Matthew 28:20). If we walk in God's ways, then all will go well with us. It is when we stray from the narrow path that we need to be concerned (Jeremiah 7:23). God has promised to write His commands on our hearts and ensure that our minds are full of His precepts (Jeremiah 31:33). If we meditate on the word of God day and night, scripture will become embedded into our thinking (Joshua 1:8). We can protect our hearts and minds from the evils of this world by thinking about the good things in life (Philippians 4:8). Set our minds on heavenly things for our life is hidden in Christ from the evil one (Colossians 3:1-3). God will then give us an undivided heart and remove from our hearts the stone-cold nature that we had before we came to God (Ezekiel 11:19-20). God is looking for people who are totally dedicated to Him and who do not let impurities come between them and God (Ezekiel 20:5-7). God has promised that, regardless of the challenges we face each day, we will never be shamed or humiliated (Joel 2:27).

There is something deep inside of us that thirsts after God. The closer we get to Him, the closer we want to be. His desire, above all else, is to be at one with us, and if we are really honest, we want to be at one with Him.

God's greatest desire is that we may be **HIS PEOPLE**. That we and HE may be one. **THINK ABOUT THAT FOR A MINUTE**. It's exciting to be a part of God's most treasured possession. The thing he values the most in all of the universe. That's those who love him and respond to HIS call. The challenge for us is that if we change direction or are always careful to stay on the narrow path among the traumas and challenges of life in the 21st century, we can enjoy close fellowship with the Lord - today and every day (Revelation 3:21). He will come in and eat with us. That is His desire, and He is right outside the door to our hearts right now. *"To him who overcomes, I will give the right to sit with me on my throne."* Do we grasp, as Christians, our position in God's family? We have an opportunity to rule with Christ to share in His glory and His sovereign power.

That is exciting, **BUT** there is more.

Revelation 21 has this to say: *"Then I saw a new heaven and a new earth, for the first heaven and the first earth had passed away, and there was no longer any sea. I saw the Holy City, the new Jerusalem coming down out of heaven from God, prepared as a bride beautifully dressed for her husband. And I heard a loud voice from the throne saying, "Now the dwelling of God is with men, and I will be their God. They will be his people, and God Himself will be with them and be their God"* Remember the covenant formula: I will be their God, and they will be my people dwelling in a new Heaven and a new earth.

God's treasured possession

God chose us to be part of His treasure. We don't deserve it; we can't earn it. We simply have to get on our knees and humbly accept it. God, in His great wisdom and mercy, chose you and me. God, who is vast and could have anything that He wanted, chose you and me to be His treasure. Do you feel God is close today? He is as close as you'll allow him to be. The Almighty creator of all the heavens of all space and time has chosen you to be His possession. To be set aside for Him. To dwell with Him for all eternity. God takes an interest in our lives (Jeremiah 29:11). God knows the plans He has for us, and they are to bring us hope and a future and are plans to bless us. We can call upon the Lord anytime. We have an open line to heaven, but God expects us to seek Him with all of our hearts, not in a lukewarm fashion but because we desire Him (Jeremiah 29:12-13).

He seeks that special relationship. He will be our God, and we will be His people: that is His desire. Have we forgotten who we are in Christ and where we are headed both in this life and in the life to come?

God's promise to all believers is this:

However, as it is written: *"No eye has seen, no ear has heard, no mind has conceived what God has prepared for those who love him, but God has revealed it to us by His Spirit."* (1 Corinthians 2:9-11 New International Version)

It is in the hands of all believers to claim that promise for our lives tonight. We should be excited about what God has planned for us as individuals of His covenant and collectively as a body of His people. We have been truly blessed by God with every spiritual blessing in the heavenly realms. God has not held anything back from us (Ephesians 1:3). The truth is that God has saved us. He has called us, and He has blessed us with everything in heaven. Do we need to remind ourselves about the vision of how wonderful our God is? How much He loves us? Nothing can separate us from the love of God, not even death or demons. Nor can anything else on this planet, or in the life yet to come, separate us from God, who is our God, and we are His people. Let us ensure that we are rooted and established in God's love to grasp how wide and long and high and deep the love of Christ is. Know that love which surpasses knowledge so that we may be filled with all the fullness of God (Ephesians 3:17-19).

God loves us. You are His treasured possession. Let us get excited by the depth of His love for us; let us press on to be filled with all the fullness that He has to give us.

Prayer

Dear Heavenly Father, thank You that You are my God and I am your child. Thank You that before the earth was formed, You created me, and among all of Your creations, I am unique; there is no one like me. Thank You, Father, that I am holy because You say that I am holy, and whenever I focus upon You, my old life simply melts away. Father God, help me to always separate myself from the world so that I can be totally devoted to You. Dear Lord, help me to grasp how awesome, pure and wonderful You are. I don't have anyone in heaven apart from You, God, and there is nothing that I desire upon the earth. Thank You, Lord, that You have hidden me from the evil one, and I can rely upon You for my daily protection. Thank You, Father, that in all things, I am more than a conqueror through Christ who died for me. Help me to always meditate on YYour wonderful deeds and, whenever time allows, to think about Your majesty. Most of all, Father, thank You that I am part of Your treasured possession and that I am highly valued by You. In Jesus's name, we pray, Amen.

Jesus in all his glory

Jesus is coming back soon. He will come on the clouds, and every eye will see Him, even those who sent Jesus to the cross and all the kingdoms and tribes of the earth will cry out because of Him (Revelation 1:7). After His resurrection, Jesus exhibited certain characteristics that He could not perform before His death.[68] For example, being able to walk out of a locked room. The scars from the nail prints in His hands and feet and the wound from the spear in His side, that He received on the cross, were present in His resurrection body. After His resurrection, Jesus was able to eat food and could be touched and physically held. Jesus was recognised by His disciples, and His resurrection body was made of flesh and bones (Luke 24:39-40).[69] After His resurrection, Jesus was not limited by time or space or by physical barriers as He was able to enter locked rooms (Luke 24:36).[70] Christ was also able to appear and disappear at will. The glory of Jesus was hidden from mankind until after His ascension into heaven and His appearance to Stephen at the time of his martyrdom and to the Apostle John in Revelation.[71] Our hope as

---

68   John F. Walvoord. Jesus Christ Our Lord, page 202. Moody Press, Chicago, USA.1969.
69   Walvoord, IBID, pages 202-203.
70   Walvoord, IBID, pages 203-204.
71   Walvoord, IBID, pages 204-205.

believers in Christ is that when we meet Him, we will be like Him and manifest a body that mirrors Christ in all his glory.[72]

Whether we find ourselves in heaven or hell is dependent on whether Jesus is our Lord and Saviour or not. Everyone who calls upon the name of the Lord shall be saved (Romans 10:13 and Joel 2:32). For those who believe and are chosen, the boundary lines have fallen for us in pleasant places, and we have an abundant heritage from God (Psalm 16:6). Believers are the beloved of God, His treasured possession, the glorious ones in whom God delights (Psalm 16:3). The gate of heaven is opened to all believers in Christ, and at a time when we are threatened with obliteration through nuclear war, then Jesus is an ever-present help in times of trouble. We can look forward to the path of life, a fullness of joy and pleasures for all of eternity (Psalm 16:11). Our belief in Jesus has brought us to the path of life, a place where we cannot be removed or hindered and an eternity of blessings. We have overcome the sting of death and are victorious over the grave (1 Corinthians 15:55-57).

God is all we have in heaven and all that we need on earth (Psalm 73:25). When we consider heaven, there is a voice standing before us saying, *"Come up here and see the splendour of my throne."* (Revelation 4:1) Holy, holy, holy is the Lord God Almighty (Revelation 4:8). God never changes; He is the same in the past, in the present and in the future. In a changing world, He is the one true standard, the one who we can rely upon forever. Heaven is a place of great rejoicing, praise and worship, as can be seen from the book of Revelation 4, 5 and 19.

---

72   Walvoord, IBID, pages 204-205.

In heaven, each child of God will recognise ourselves as an infinitely beloved child of God who is transformed into the likeness of Christ.[73]

Resurrection

As believers in Christ as our Lord and Saviour, we are waiting for Jesus to come back and claim us as his bride: the church (Revelation 19:7; 21:2). The Bible sees the church as the purified bride of Christ, holy and spotless. We, as believers in Christ, will be resurrected to be with him, and, it must be clear, the Bible describes the resurrection of mankind in several stages and different groups:

1. Believers at the time of the rapture. When Christ returns in the clouds, they will be resurrected to be with him. Those who have fallen asleep (the dead) in Christ will be resurrected first. Almost immediately, those who are still alive will be transported to the clouds to be with the Lord (1 Thessalonians 4:14-17).

2. Israel and the Old Testament saints. At the time of Jesus's coming to earth to establish his kingdom, this will be a separate group who are resurrected (Daniel 12:2; Hosea 13:14; Matthew 22:30-32).[74]

3. Christians who have come to faith through tribulation. This is a distinct group who are resurrected at the end of time (Revelation 20:4).

---

73 Bruce Milne. The Message of Heaven and Hell. Chapter 4. Long may he live, page 87. InterVarsity Press, Leicester, UK. 2002

74 John F. Walvoord. *Jesus Christ Our Lord. The future work of Christ is also dependent on his resurrection*, pp. 215-216. Moody Bible Institute, Chicago, USA, 1969.

4.   The wicked and those who have chosen darkness over Christ. This final group faces God's anger and will be resurrected for judgement at the end of time/millennial reign of Christ (Revelation 20:12-14).[75]

The Bible describes mankind as being made up of a body, soul and spirit (1 Thessalonians 5:23). Paul prays that God will sanctify our body, soul and spirit so that we will be faultless at the coming of Jesus (1 Thessalonians 5:23-24).

Heaven and earth

Once we reach heaven, all our suffering, trials and tribulations will be behind us. We will be delivered from past iniquities and painful memories (Isaiah 65:17). Thankfully, there will be a new heaven, a new earth, and a new Jerusalem (Isaiah 66:22 and Revelation 21:1-11), which is most welcome when we consider how mankind has effectively brought such great destruction on the present earth.

The Bible describes in some detail the paradise which will be found in the new Jerusalem (Revelation 21:15-21). The glory of God will shine down upon the city, and there will be no need for a temple or a church building to go and worship in because God himself will be inside the heart of every believer. The glory of God will light up the whole universe, and we will all experience the immenseness of God's glory that the universe will shine brighter than any star. The beauty is that God is light, and where God is, there can be no darkness (1 John 1:5). Therefore, the new heaven and the new earth will never grow dark because God's light reigns forever (Revelation

---

75   IBID.

21:22-24). Believers in Christ will form the heavenly body of Christ, and we will worship God in Spirit and in truth.

Paradise in heaven

There will be no more suffering or striving to make ends meet because we shall be in paradise. Every tear will be wiped away, and there will be no more grief, mourning or pain (Revelation 21:4). There will be no more hunger or thirst and no need to toil under the midday sun to make ends meet (Revelation 7:16-17). Death and humiliation will be a thing of the past, never to be experienced again (Isaiah 25:8).

The purity and holiness of God will be seen by everyone who is in heaven as we stand before God on His throne, ruling the universe. God's throne is surrounded by creatures and elders who continually fall down in worship and awe of God (Revelation 4:4-11). There will be a great multitude of Christians, full of holiness and far too many to count, who have been saved and resurrected through their belief in Jesus (Revelation 7:1-17). We must ensure that we are among the elect of Christ and members of God's family. The ark of the covenant will be seen in heaven (Revelation 11:19). There will be much rejoicing and worshipping of God for all that he has done in redeeming mankind and bringing believers to eternal life in him (Revelation 19:1-8).

Jesus declares that the Kingdom of Heaven is like a wedding banquet and that many were invited. However, a number of those invited refused to come or were too busy to come to the feast (Matthew 22:1-13). Earthly pursuits should not get in the way of a heavenly calling, and who among us does not like a good wedding? To enter the heavenly party and to be a part of the banquet, we must dress appropriately and put on a robe of righteousness. Those who do not have the robe will be bound up and thrown outside into the darkness that is hell (Matthew 22:13). Those who are righteous in God's sight can enter the Kingdom of God. Our filthy rags will be removed from us, and we will be clothed in heavenly garments that show our purity and holiness (Zechariah 3:3-4, Isaiah 1:18). Those who overcome the trials and tribulations of life and call upon the name of the Lord will receive salvation, and we can look at our names written in God's Book of Life (Revelation 3:5).

Our Father's house

Jesus has prepared our dwelling place in God's mansion in heaven (John 14:1-3).[76] There is no need to be weighed down by the trials of this world because we can focus on heavenly things and our place in God's mansion. This world is not our home or final resting place; paradise awaits. We should ensure we have treasure in heaven because we will all want to have something wonderful to put in our rooms (Matthew 6:20).[77] We are requested to do what is correct by caring for the poor, the widows and orphans (Isaiah 1:17). We are considered faultless and pure if we have regard for widows and orphans and by not being polluted by what the world has to offer (James 1:27). We should focus and consider helping the hungry, the thirsty, those who are poor and homeless. These attributes separate the righteous from the wicked (Matthew 25:31-46).

76　Roger Ellsworth. *What the Bible Teaches About Heaven*, pp. 79-85. Evangelical Press, Darlington, UK, 2007.

77　IBID, pages 107-114.

The new Jerusalem

The new Jerusalem will shine with the glory of God, and its appearance will be crystal clear. It will be huge in comparison to any city we currently see on the earth, some 1,400 miles long and the same distance wide (Revelation 21:10-27). The river of life will flow through the middle of the city, and the tree of life grows on both banks of the river (Revelation 22:1-5). The city will be covered in precious stones and lined with gold, and there will be no darkness, so the gates will always be open for us to come and go as God wishes. The city also contains the great thrones of God and Jesus, from which the Godhead rule the cosmos (Revelation 22:3). Although men have tried to describe the glorious sight of God's throne, words fail to meet the majesty and beauty that is found in heaven (Ezekiel 1:26-28; Daniel 7:9-14; Revelation 4:2-11). The elect will experience the glory of God and participate in the worship services that are in heaven. Hallelujah, we beseech You to come soon Lord Jesus.

𝕻𝖗𝖆𝖞𝖊𝖗[78]

Dear Heavenly Father, thank You so much that we are part of Your family. Praise You that one day we will be in heaven with You and that all our trials and tribulations will be behind us. Thank You that there will be a day when we will be able to participate in the worship services in heaven and enjoy our room in Your mansion. Thank you, Father, that You will wipe away every tear and replace our tears with rejoicing and blessings beyond what we could ever hope or imagine. Thank You, Lord Jesus, that You are coming soon for Your children to take us to our heavenly homes. Above all, thank You, Father, that we will be able to experience the new Jerusalem, to see the golden streets, to walk next to the river of life and to eat the fruit from the tree of life. Thank You so much. In Jesus's name, we pray, Amen.

---

78   John Clarke. Faithful God 2022. Lightning Source Publishers, Milton Keynes, UK. page 139

Other books available

The book explores seven key areas to the victorious Christian life and remaining free in Christ regardless of the circumstances we find ourselves facing in the coming days. As Christians, we are either afraid of or want to skip over quickly the challenging teachings in the word of God, such as the struggles with and consequences of sin, and the coming wrath of God, in order to reach the more positive teachings on salvation and eternal life for all who believe in Jesus as Lord and Saviour.

All of us want to be free from the things that hold us captive in life. Jesus offered us the opportunity to know the truth, and that his truth would set us free. Totally free means being set free to be the person God created us to be, to be free from fear, circumstances, or the strongholds that tell us that we can never achieve all that we want to achieve. The Bible is the only source of the truth that promises to set us free. This book explores the principles and defines the tenets that allow us to be set free from the strongholds that bind us and try to limit us to less than we are capable of achieving in this life. The book outlines some of the major obstacles that bind us and stop us from being free. The book also indicates how we can find the freedom that

Jesus promised through the truth of the Gospel. The book explores twelve areas of the truth of the Christian life and outlines some of the principles needed to remain free in Christ, regardless of the circumstances we find ourselves facing.

The book provides an overview of who God is and why we can rely upon Him, regardless of the circumstances we find ourselves facing. A clearer understanding of the living God and His awesome power to deliver and rescue us from a world that is out of control, and becoming darker as we move towards the end of this age, will help us all to stand firm and know that God has plans for each of us. Those plans will give hope and a future and show that God's ultimate purpose is to bring us into a closer, more profound and deeper relationship with Him.

About the Author

John Clarke is an Evangelical Christian based in Wokingham, Berkshire, England. He has lived in Liverpool, Southampton, Guildford, Reading, Macclesfield and Wokingham in England and Milan in Italy. He has extensive writing experience, having written four books, contributed to seven other books, and published over 80 papers in peer-reviewed journals. John has been a lay preacher for over 40 years.

www.ingramcontent.com/pod-product-compliance
Lightning Source LLC
Chambersburg PA
CBHW012015050726

47590CB00009B/3192